TEACHING ADULTS

A Literacy Resource Book

New Readers Press®
ProLiteracy's publishing division

Acknowledgments

This book is the result of the work and collaboration of many people. It also builds on the work done by literacy practitioners across the country. Pat Bleakley, Linda Church, Margaret Hampstead, Jane Hugo, and Wendy Stein worked on the original research and manuscript. Amy Wilson researched, revised, and brought the book up-to-date. Dr. Betty Aderman shared her library and her reading expertise. Jane MacKillop and Lydia Wallace provided particular help with the sections on development and assessment of portfolios. Twyla Ferguson, Dr. Alton Greenfield, Barbara Burks Hanley, Lorraine Loitz, Dr. Mary Dunn Siedow, Linda Church, and Dr. Alisa Belzer gave helpful comments as content reviewers.

Teaching Adults: A Literacy Resource Book
ISBN 978-1-56420-343-4

Copyright © 2013, 2003, 1994 New Readers Press
New Readers Press
ProLiteracy's Publishing Division
104 Marcellus Street, Syracuse, New York 13204
www.newreaderspress.com

Printed in the United States of America
9   8   7   6   5   4

Proceeds from the sale of New Readers Press materials support professional development, training, and technical assistance programs of ProLiteracy that benefit local literacy programs in the U.S. and around the globe.

Developmental Editor: Terrie Lipke
Design and Production Director: James Wallace
Technology Specialist: Maryellen Casey
Senior Designer: Carolyn Wallace

Contents

Introduction

Lack of basic literacy skills is an issue that affects people not just in the United States but also around the world. Though estimates vary, most major surveys say that at least 30 million Americans aged 16 and over cannot read and write beyond the fifth-grade level. Approximately 63 million—29 percent of U.S. adults—cannot read well enough to understand a newspaper story written at the eighth-grade level. The effects of illiteracy go beyond just limiting educational opportunities. Adults need basic literacy skills in order to get good jobs so they can provide for themselves and their families, to be healthy and raise healthy children, to be active members of their communities, and to navigate the technology that is increasingly part of their everyday lives.

ProLiteracy's individual members and member programs offer adults instruction in basic literacy, English as a second or other language, math, and GED® test preparation. Thousands of volunteer tutors, professional educators, and adult new readers themselves are working to improve the lives of adults through the power of literacy.

This Book

Teaching Adults: A Literacy Resource Book is designed to provide tutors and teachers with knowledge and instructional tools to meet the diverse needs of learners. It pulls together many of the best instructional strategies that have been proven effective for helping adults improve their literacy skills. It includes background information on literacy as well as 80 specific activities that tutors can use with literacy learners.

Reading research reveals that instruction and activities in these four key areas are important to helping learners improve reading skills:

1. Fluency: reading with efficiency and ease

2. Alphabetics: linking sounds with letters, phonemic awareness, and word analysis skills

3. Vocabulary: understanding the meaning of words

4. Comprehension: constructing meaning from text

In this book, you will find easy-to-use instructional activities organized around each of these areas.

Tutoring

This resource is for you to use to supplement and add planned activities to your instruction. Whether you are just beginning to tutor adults or you have tutored for many years, *Teaching Adults: A Literacy Resource Book* will provide you with both guidance and concrete activities to support students' learning goals. To connect with a local literacy organization, access the ProLiteracy website at www.proliteracy.org or the National Literacy Directory at www.nationalliteracydirectory.org.

The material in this book expresses ProLiteracy's commitment to the following beliefs.

Each Adult Learner Is a Unique Individual

Adult learners bring a wealth of knowledge and experiences to the learning process. Each adult learner is a unique individual with his or her own needs and interests. This idea is at the core of teaching adults. In order to ensure success, the tutor or teacher must work with the learner to customize the program to the learner's interests, long-term goals, and short-term objectives.

Another important point to remember is that adult learners lead busy lives and often have many responsibilities. Be prepared to make every minute of every lesson count.

Tutoring Is Effective

Traditional instructional methods failed many of the adults in literacy programs. Tutoring, whether one-to-one or in small groups, offers a unique opportunity. Tutors can develop a respectful and encouraging relationship with learners and create a new environment for learning. In this new environment, tutors trained in basic instructional techniques and learning theory can guide and support a learner's literacy development.

Reading and Writing Are Meaning-Based Processes

The goal of literacy instruction is to help learners gain the skills, knowledge, and attitudes needed to actively make meaning out of written language—to see themselves as capable readers and writers.

To make meaning, people must be able to do the following:

- Recognize the language forms (e.g., letters, words, styles, and formats) in what they read and use these forms in what they write.

- Understand the author's purpose for writing and have a purpose for what they themselves write.

- Respond to, connect with, and form opinions about what they read using their prior knowledge about the topic, their experiences, and their values, and expect others to do the same with what they write.

- Apply the meanings they make to their lives.

A Variety of Instructional Approaches Is Needed

Teacher and researcher Marilyn Gillespie tells us, "Literacy is the 'exercised' ability to use reading and writing to get information one needs and to exchange it with others. This implies that learners must connect literacy to its meaning in their everyday lives and find ways to determine for themselves the conditions under which they will use reading and writing. It means there is not just one literacy, decided on by experts, but 'many literacies,' defined by each of us, individually and together" (Marilyn Gillespie, *Many Literacies: Modules for Training Adult Beginning Readers and Tutors*, Amherst, MA: Center for International Education, 1990, p. 2). This suggests that no one instructional approach or published series can address all the ways different adults will use their literacy skills. Consequently, tutors need to be able to use a variety of teaching techniques and materials. They need to understand the following concepts:

- Listening, speaking, reading, and writing are interrelated parts of the language acquisition process. Instruction in reading and writing should allow learners to integrate all four of these communication modes and to become active, flexible, and independent communicators of ideas and feelings.

- Literacy instruction should help learners increase their capacity to participate in their communities and families and to use their skills to improve the world in which they live.

- Literacy instruction should take into account the personal feelings, needs, and concerns of learners. It should aim to overcome any sense of past failure related to learning, to encourage risk taking, and to enable learners to reach specific goals.

- Literacy instruction should be based on learner assessment. Assessment should be a shared and ongoing process that helps ensure that learning programs meet learners' goals and objectives.

- Literacy instruction is more effective when learners help identify objectives and specific activities, are guided by the tutors during the activities, and reflect on the learning afterward. This process enables learners to tie instruction to their needs, experience success during instruction, and recognize what progress they have made.

ProLiteracy

ProLiteracy, a nonprofit organization based in Syracuse, New York, champions the power of literacy to improve the lives of adults and their families, communities, and societies. It works with adult new readers and learners and with local and national organizations to help adults gain the reading, writing, math, computer, and English language skills they need to be successful. ProLiteracy advocates on behalf of adult learners and the programs that serve them, provides training and professional development, and publishes materials used in adult literacy and basic education instruction. It has 1,100 member programs in all 50 states and the District of Columbia, and it works with 50 partners in 34 developing countries. ProLiteracy was created in 2002 through the merger of Laubach Literacy International and Literacy Volunteers of America, Inc. ProLiteracy's publishing division, New Readers Press, publishes materials used by literacy instructors and programs.

Find out more about ProLiteracy and how you can become a member at http://www.proliteracy.org. You will also be able to access information about our trainer certification program and our online professional development courses. To look at the New Readers Press online catalog, go to http://www.newreaderspress.com.

For More Help: ProLiteracy Education Network

ProLiteracy has a special website for tutors, teachers, and program managers who are working with adult literacy or ESL (English as a second language) learners. The site is called ProLiteracy Education Network or simply EdNet. It contains free resources designed to help you improve the services you provide. You can access it at http://www.ProLiteracyEdnet.org.

If you are a tutor or teacher, you can take our short online courses to learn new teaching techniques or to learn more about the ones described in this book. You can also find information about a variety of topics such as teaching citizenship, creating a teaching toolbox, or using technology in your lessons. You can download reading selections with student exercises, or you can help a student select a story that has an optional audio component so he or she can practice skills outside the classroom. ProLiteracy continues to add new resources to this site, so plan to visit frequently.

Adult Literacy

What Is Literacy?

At one time, people who could sign their names and recognize simple words were considered literate. In today's complex society, daily life and work demand a much higher level of reading and writing. A modern definition of literacy must acknowledge these increased demands. It must also acknowledge literacy as a tool—a means to an end—rather than the end itself.

As literacy demands have become more complex, so too have definitions of literacy. More recently, literacy has come to be recognized as having multiple definitions specific to the individual, his or her uses of it, and the social setting in which it is practiced. Recent definitions reflect this multi-literacy perspective. The 2003 National Assessment of Adult Literacy (NAAL) includes a definition of literacy that targets the tasks adults need to accomplish as well as the knowledge and literacy skills they need to accomplish those tasks.

The 2003 NAAL's task-based definition of literacy is this: "the ability to use printed and written information to function in society, to achieve one's goals, and to develop one's knowledge and potential." And the definition explains the required skills this way: "successful use of printed material is a product of two classes of skills—word-level reading skills and higher level literacy skills." This definition does not tie literacy to one standard ability or grade level but recognizes that literacy is related to the needs of each individual.

Adult Literacy in the United States

Over the years, there have been many different definitions of literacy. Therefore, estimates of the extent of illiteracy in the United States differ. The need for adult literacy education includes Americans whose first language is English and Americans for whom English is acquired as a second or other language. The following are some of the results of the major studies that have attempted to measure adult illiteracy and its effects in this country:

- 2001: According to the American Management Association Survey on Workplace Testing, 34.1% of applicants tested by respondent firms lacked the basic skills necessary to perform the jobs they sought. And 84.6% of the respondent firms did not hire skill-deficient applicants.

- 2003: The National Assessment of Adult Literacy found that 75% of food stamp recipients performed in the lowest two literacy levels. Of welfare recipients, 90% were high school dropouts.

- 2003: The Bush administration's "Literacy in Everyday Life—Results From the 2003 National Assessment of Adult Literacy" determined that 43% of adults age 16 and over read at the basic or below-basic level, 44% read at the intermediate level, and 13% were defined as proficient.

- 2003: Of all juveniles who interfaced with the juvenile court system, 85% were functionally illiterate. More than 56% of all prison inmates read at the basic or below-basic level. Records showed that inmates had a 16% chance of returning to prison if they received literacy help as opposed to a 70% chance if they received no help. (National Assessment of Adult Literacy)

- 2006: About 82% of children whose parents had less than a high school diploma lived in low-income families. (National Center for Children in Poverty)

- 2009: A Columbia University study predicted a shortage of 7 million properly educated workers by 2012. The same study reported other troubling numbers like a $192 billion total loss in potential wages from workers without a high school diploma.

- 2012: Every year one in four young adults—about 1 million people—drops out of high school. (Building a Grad Nation Report)

Literacy tutors, teachers, and learners across the country are working in community centers, schools, workplaces, churches, family literacy programs, prisons, libraries, and homeless shelters to make adult literacy instruction a priority and to make adult literacy a reality.

True Stories: Stories of New Readers

Profiles in Persistence and Perseverance

There are many inspiring stories about people whose lives have been changed by literacy. The story of Melissa Stoner (learner) and Sharon Buehrer (tutor) is a story I'd like to share with everyone.

A young mother of young children, Melissa desperately wanted to obtain her GED certificate. She had dropped out of high school to work to help support her family financially. Over the years, while struggling with serious health issues and declining vision, she knew she wanted to earn her GED so that she could better provide for her children. Then Melissa found the Learning Center at the James V. Brown Library in Williamsport, PA, directed by Linda Herr.

A student at the local Catholic High School decided to volunteer at the Learning Center for his senior project, and he asked Sharon Buehrer, the school librarian, to mentor his senior project. They went to volunteer tutor training together. Sharon wasn't sure if she could teach someone to read and write, but she remembered a scene in an Indiana Jones movie when Jones took a leap of faith. So she bravely stepped out and decided to take the leap. Sharon was retiring soon, and she wanted to tutor an adult.

Sharon was paired up with her new student, Melissa. For more than three years Melissa met with Sharon once or twice every week. Melissa studied and learned and never gave up. Health problems interrupted her and caused delays, but she held on to her goal of obtaining her GED. Melissa said that failure was not a motivation for her, and she wouldn't use excuses to quit. She said that her tutor, Sharon, listened and used her interests to help her to stay focused. Sharon was patient and had a real "stick with it" attitude. Melissa said her children kept her positive, her responsibilities kept her positive, and Sharon kept her positive. Her final hurdle was to learn the intimidating math she needed to pass the GED math test. Would she be able to do it?

Sharon said that math wasn't her strong subject but that she'd do her best to help Melissa. As they began working on the required math, the Learning Center's funding was eliminated by the Pennsylvania Department of Education. Both women remained strong. Sharon said that staying connected to the program was important to her. She had received additional training there and had bounced ideas off the professional staff. She hoped that the program would stay open.

Melissa needed a flexible tutoring schedule and the one-on-one tutoring program provided that for her. The program was personalized, and the library environment was positive. Finally, after much hard work, Melissa made the call to Linda Herr: She had passed the math test and the other four GED tests! Melissa celebrated and shared her joy with her children.

Now Melissa is exploring job opportunities and volunteering with the Shepherd of the Streets programs. She and Sharon went out to lunch to honor their partnership and determination. With persistence and perseverance, both Melissa and Sharon achieved their goals.

(Amy Wilson, Mid-State Literacy Council, State College, Pennsylvania, 2012.)

Reading Helps Me Reach for the Stars

How did it all come about for me? When my stepdaughter was in kindergarten, it hit me like a ton of bricks. "Oh, no!" I thought to myself. I can't read or write very well. What am I going to do when she gets into the higher grades and asks me to help her with her homework? Of course, that day came. Like all illiterate people we have ways to get around any situation. I would tell her your daddy can help you with that. He's better at spelling and math than I am. Well I got around that one, I thought.

Being illiterate stayed on my mind a lot. I just didn't know where to go to get help. I wouldn't tell my husband, because he had no idea. He always thought I just dropped out of high school. He never asked what grade I dropped out of, so it was never talked about.

One day I decided to stop by the library on the way home from work. Walking up to the desk where the librarian was standing, I asked her if they had a program to help people who can't read. The librarian gave me a phone number to call. Of course I called it, and what did I get but an answering machine, which at that time I wouldn't talk on. I just hung up.

Shortly after that I was at work and some of the girls were talking about going back to night school to get their GED. They said, "Why don't you go back to school with us?" I thought I would die, for I couldn't let them know that the GED wasn't what I needed. So I decided maybe if I studied hard enough I could do it anyway. So I gave it a good try. I would stay up half the night trying to do my books, going to bed at 2:00 a.m. and getting up at 5:00 a.m. to go to work. I was also trying to visit my mother three days a week in a nursing home. Going to school two nights a week, doing all my housework, it didn't take long before I was burned out. My husband told me I had to quit school, so I did.

One day I was home alone, I decided to watch TV awhile. I turned it on, and there I was watching a story about a man who couldn't read or write. As I watched the story I saw myself. The trouble he was having and things he was going through were like me. At the end of the story they put a number on the TV screen. I wrote it on a piece of paper. Later when I was by myself, I called it. A lady named Nancy talked with me on the phone and set up an appointment for me to come and see her. Nancy told me how to get there and where I had to go. When I got there I was scared to death, my hands were shaking, and my knees were knocking. After I talked to Nancy awhile, I wasn't scared anymore. She took down the information she needed. She told me they would call me when they found me a tutor.

My goals in life now are so different than they were two years ago. Now I can use a dictionary and read a road map, balance a checkbook, and even write checks out and spell the numbers right. I can read a newspaper and use the phone book to look up phone numbers. But most of all I like reading because I can read a book and understand it.

I love reading very much. Now my goal is to get my GED and become a veterinary assistant. Most of all I want to tell people who can't read or write there is a rainbow. Reading to me is like finding the pot of gold at the end of the rainbow.

(By Maybelle Biggerstaff, from *Not by Myself . . .*, Literacy South, 1992. Used by permission.)

Not Being Able to Read

I will always be scared of someone finding out I cannot read. I do not understand people today or in high school. When I was in high school I went from class to class and grade to grade not being able to read. Do you think the teachers knew or cared that I could not read? I don't believe they cared; if they did, why didn't they say something?

Today I can read better, and I enjoy reading. Sometimes I get so frustrated when I cannot read or spell something. It's that one word that gets me. I am a quiet person, and I think it is because of the way I read. Today reading is a big part of my life. If people know you can't read well or at all they will call you dumb.

I looked for two years for someone to teach me to read. I did not ask for help reading in school because I was afraid people would call me dumb or worthless. My tutor is a wonderful teacher to work with me week in and week out. I am thankful for her, and I will never forget her. I like going to class, but I know one day it will end.

I hope one day the frustration will be gone, but I will not give up. This quiet person lives on. I hope one day someone will understand what I'm saying about reading.

What is it like to read or spell something without getting frustrated? Maybe one day I will know.

(By The Bird, from *Not By Myself . . .*, Literacy South, 1992. Used by permission.)

Adults as Learners

The Stories of New Readers section makes it clear that literacy volunteers teach people, not books or skills. When you teach adults, you need to consider the following:

- Characteristics and needs of adult learners in general and new readers in particular

- Special needs

- Individual learning preferences

General Characteristics and Needs of Adult Learners

Learning to read as an adult is different in many ways from learning as a child. To be an effective tutor or teacher, you'll need to understand what adults are like and what they need and want in a learning situation. The chart below and on the next page sums up some important characteristics of adult learners (not just new readers) and the implications for teaching.

Adult learners	As a tutor or teacher, you should
want and deserve respect	give frequent praise and support emphasize the skills and strengths the learner already has design lessons so that the learner experiences success believe in the learner and his or her ability to learn treat tutoring as a partnership between equals use the learner's first name only if you invite the learner to use your first name and he or she is comfortable doing so

Adult learners	As a tutor or teacher, you should
are used to making decisions	involve the learner in setting goals and objectives offer choices of activities and materials ask the learner to evaluate the lessons respect the learner's priorities and opinions
are busy people	develop lesson plans that address priority needs use the tutoring time efficiently be flexible in assigning homework help the learner schedule homework time
have to deal with emergencies and unexpected situations	make an agreement to call if either you or the learner cannot make it to a session have alternative activities ready in case the learner did not have time to prepare for the planned lesson
have a wealth of life experiences	build self-esteem by emphasizing how much the learner already knows or can do be open to what the learner can teach you design instructional activities around the learner's work, community, family, politics, hobbies, friends, or current interests
sometimes feel insecure about using new skills on their own	provide plenty of opportunities to practice new skills practice an exercise with the learner before asking the learner to do it alone or for homework provide support, such as audio recordings of a reading assignment encourage the learner to use computer programs (where available) to reinforce skills emphasize the learner's progress don't ask a question if you know the learner doesn't know the answer
have their own values and beliefs	respect the learner's values and don't try to change them don't judge
may have special physical needs	be sensitive to possible sight or hearing problems provide adequate lighting speak clearly meet in a place that is comfortable and accessible to the learner provide adequate break time
want to apply what they learn to their present lives	find out what the learner's needs are show how a skill or lesson helps the learner move closer to meeting those needs

Characteristics of Adult New Readers

Adult new readers share the characteristics of all adult learners. Adult new readers might also have some of the needs or characteristics listed in the chart below.

Adult new readers	As a tutor or teacher, you should
may fear school or classroom situations	find out what school experiences were unpleasant for the learner, and avoid re-creating them
	stress what the learner has done right
	avoid criticizing or ridiculing the learner
	sit next to, rather than stand over, the learner
	de-emphasize formal testing
may have problems meeting basic needs because of unemployment or poverty	refer the learner to an appropriate source of assistance if the learner wants help
may be embarrassed or ashamed about being unable to read and write	reassure the learner that many adults are in the same situation
	encourage the learner to attend a student support group, if your program has one
	be supportive and let the learner know there is nothing wrong with him or her
	find a private place for lessons if the learner is uncomfortable working in a public area

Special Needs

Hearing and Vision Problems

Older people often begin to experience problems with hearing or sight. In addition, many adult new readers do not have access to regular health care and may have problems that have never been diagnosed. Others may not be able to afford new glasses or other services they need. Below are signs that you should look for and suggestions for what you can do if you detect a problem.

Hearing problems: The learner may tell you that he or she has a hearing problem, or you may discover it through observation. Notice if the learner speaks loudly, often asks you to repeat yourself, misunderstands you, or turns an ear toward you when you speak.

If these things happen, you can

- enunciate clearly

- speak loudly without yelling

- make sure the learner is looking at you when you start to speak

- ask the learner to repeat explanations or instructions so you can check understanding

- speak slowly

- recommend that the learner have a hearing check

Keep in mind that some learners may have had hearing problems since early childhood. Such problems may have affected their ability to develop and use language effectively. As a result, they may also have had problems learning to read.

Vision problems: Signs of vision problems include squinting, holding a book very close or very far away, bending low over the table, experiencing headaches and eye fatigue, being unable to read small print, and misreading words. If you suspect vision problems, you can

- ask the learner to tell you if the print is too small

- work in a well-lighted area

- use large-print books, enlarge the text by using a photocopy machine, or use electronic files and enlarge the text on a computer screen or tablet

- use a magnifying bar

- recommend that the learner have an eye exam

- find out if a group in your area (such as the Lions Club) can help provide glasses for people who can't afford them

Some people with 20/20 vision have other kinds of vision problems that can interfere with learning to read. For example, a person might have difficulty with binocular vision (using both eyes together). Dr. Dale Jordan, a learning disabilities specialist from Oklahoma City, suggests that tutors and teachers observe the learner for the following signs, which may indicate other vision problems.

Notice if the learner tends to

- hold the pencil in a "funny" way (if right-handed)

- put his or her head on the desk to read

- slump in the chair

- close one eye

- develop a headache after only a few minutes of reading

- complain of tired eyes

- confuse right and left

- have difficulty looking steadily at the work

- fidget

- have watery eyes

- yawn a lot

- skip or reverse words or letters

Learning Differences and Learning Disabilities

Not everyone who has trouble learning to read has a learning disability. However, researchers suggest that between 50 and 80 percent of adults in literacy programs display characteristics typical of individuals with learning disabilities (Nightingale, 1991). The term *learning disabilities* refers to a broad spectrum of processing disorders that arise from problems taking in, storing, retrieving, or expressing information.

The definition of learning disabilities adopted by the National Joint Committee on Learning Disabilities in 1990 is as follows:

> Learning disabilities is a general term that refers to a heterogeneous group of disorders manifested by significant difficulties in the acquisition and use of listening, speaking, reading, writing, reasoning, or mathematical abilities. These disorders are intrinsic to the individual, presumed to be due to central nervous system dysfunction, and may occur across the life span. Problems in self-regulatory behaviors, social perception, and social interaction may exist with learning disabilities but do not by themselves constitute a learning disability. Although learning disabilities may occur concomitantly with other handicapping conditions (for example, sensory impairment, mental retardation, serious emotional disturbance), or with extrinsic influences (such as cultural differences, insufficient or inappropriate instruction), they are not the result of those conditions or influences.

Learning disabilities reflect a discrepancy between a person's ability and performance levels. The person usually has at least average intelligence. The measurement of ability and performance can be particularly frustrating for a teacher because results are often inconsistent. A learner may demonstrate high to very high aptitude and achievement in one area; in another area, results may indicate below average to very low achievement. In literacy programs, adults with learning disabilities may exhibit a wide range of proficiency levels.

People with learning disabilities can learn to cope with these difficulties. They need to understand that their learning problems are caused by specific conditions that can be identified and addressed.

Tutors, in consultation with their literacy programs, must determine whether problems that occur in tutoring are caused by the methods of instruction or by learning disabilities. You should talk to your program director if you suspect a learner has learning disabilities. The program should seek professional help to assess the individual.

The following behaviors may indicate learning difficulties if they continue over a long period of time:

- Hyperactivity (e.g., being restless, having poor motor coordination, talking a lot but frequently with incomplete thoughts)

- Hypoactivity (e.g., reacting slowly, working slowly, seeming unemotional)

- Attention problems (e.g., daydreaming, seeming confused, having difficulty concentrating, being easily distracted)

- Impulsivity (e.g., acting without thinking and without concern for consequences, not staying with a task, saying one thing and meaning another, speaking at inappropriate times)

- Other general behaviors (e.g., misinterpreting what others say; having memory problems; being clumsy; displaying poor decision-making skills; having difficulty managing time; displaying poor fine motor skills; confusing left and right, up and down, or east and west)

If you know you are working with a learning disabled adult, try a variety of techniques to build on the learner's strengths, and try other techniques and materials when the learner is frustrated. In addition to using multisensory techniques, consider some of the following suggestions:

- Present information in very small, manageable steps.

- Structure activities.

- Provide frequent reinforcement.

- Provide frequent feedback.

- Teach new material in concrete ways. Give examples.

- Relate new material to the learner's everyday life.

- Discuss and study new vocabulary words before they appear in the instructional material.

- Experiment with large print.

- Use graph paper to help with letter spacing in writing.

- Prepare the learner for changes in routine before they occur.

- Rephrase questions during discussions and on assessments if the learner doesn't understand something.

- Make frequent eye contact. (This may be very difficult for some disabled learners.)

- Set up instructional space away from distractions (e.g., doors, windows, and heating and air conditioning units).

- Restate information in a variety of ways.

- Use a colored transparency to change the contrast between ink and paper on reading materials.

- Teach and encourage the use of mnemonics (techniques for memorizing information).

- Be well prepared for each session.

- When giving a test, make it untimed and use multiple-choice questions.

(The information in this section was taken from *A Learning Disabilities Digest for Literacy Providers*, Learning Disabilities Association of America, 1991.)

The latest research indicates that structured practice may be an effective way to help learners with reading disabilities. As reported in *Learning to Achieve* (National Institute for Literacy, 2010), "One [very important instructional] component was explicit practice, which included activities related to distributed review and practice, repeated practice, sequenced reviews, daily feedback, and/or weekly reviews."

If you're not sure which of these strategies will work best with a specific learner, ask your literacy program for assistance. The most important thing is to keep trying and ask the learner what helps him or her to learn. All learners have accomplishments, and asking them to describe to you how they learned a skill will help you to understand how to teach new skills to them. Learning may be slower and more frustrating for someone with learning disabilities, but the results can be well worth the extra effort required.

Assistive Technologies

Assistive technologies are tools or devices that increase learners' independence and support learning. Assistive technology tools can be high tech or low tech. Consult with your literacy program for help choosing assistive technology tools. Examples of assistive technologies are

- computers with adaptive software that support reading and writing

- e-readers with optional display settings

- text-to-speech programs or audio readers

- audiobooks

- audio players

- reading pens

- pencil grips

- highlighting marker tape

- earplugs

- colored overlays

Individual Learning Preferences

A learning preference is the way a person takes in, stores, and retrieves information. People differ in which of the five physical senses (hearing, sight, touch, taste, and smell) they most depend on when learning and what kind of environment helps them learn best.

PHYSICAL SENSES: PATHWAYS TO THE BRAIN

The three main senses a learner uses in developing literacy skills are hearing, sight, and touch. Many tutors find that using multisensory teaching helps the learner process information and skills.

Type of learning path	Characteristics
auditory path	learns by listening and discussing
visual path	learns by visualizing and by looking at text, charts, pictures, etc.
kinesthetic/tactile path	learns by doing and by being physically involved in a task

Each of these senses provides a different pathway for information to reach a person's brain. Some people are very strong in one pathway, while others may use two or even three pathways well. A multisensory approach to teaching and learning involves all three of these senses. It has the following advantages:

- It ensures that the tutor will provide opportunities for a learner to use the sense that works best, even if the tutor is not sure what that sense is.

- The more pathways a learner uses, the more likely he or she is to remember and retain the information.

- People tend to rely on different senses depending on the tasks at hand.

The next chart outlines some learning-style characteristics and ideas for involving each of the three senses in your teaching.

Learners who favor auditory pathways	As a tutor or teacher, you can
process most easily information they hear prefer oral instructions understand information best when they repeat it aloud after hearing it can discriminate between words that sound alike (*bet/bat*) and between similar sounds (*s/z*) can reproduce information they hear: sounds, words, grammatical structures	read to the learner make audio recordings of reading selections for the learner to use while reading encourage the learner to discuss or summarize a reading passage ask the learner to repeat instructions use oral reading techniques (see Activities 14–18) use music and rhythms to reinforce learning

Learners who favor visual pathways	As a tutor or teacher, you can
"see" information in their minds (form mental pictures) prefer written instructions or demonstrations	choose materials with pictures and other illustrations use flashcards, diagrams, and charts use language experience activities to help the learner see his or her words and ideas in print (see Activities 7–13) write instructions to reinforce oral instructions use a highlighter to call attention to key words or phrases use visualization techniques to help with spelling, sight words, and comprehension

Learners who favor kinesthetic/tactile pathways	As a tutor or teacher, you can
are physically active learn by touching and doing may recall information more easily when some physical action is involved: walking, touching objects, moving, taking notes would rather do something than talk or write about it	have the learner trace letters or words (when learning to spell) develop writing activities to reinforce the reading skills being learned ask the learner to draw a picture that represents the story use letter cards or letter game tiles to spell words use word cards to form sentences use computers or simulation and board games provide frequent breaks during sessions change activities often

Environment

Environmental factors can also influence how effectively people learn. Take the following factors into account as you and the adult learner with whom you are working consider when and where to schedule your sessions and what in your learning space is helpful or distracting.

Time of day
Some people learn better in the morning, others in the afternoon, and still others in the evening.

Setting
Some people have difficulty concentrating in their homes because there are too many distractions. Some are uncomfortable working in public areas. Some prefer a particular type of chair or a particular table height.

Length of session
Some people like to work in long uninterrupted sessions; others prefer short sessions and frequent breaks.

Involvement with others
Some people learn best alone; others prefer to work in groups.

Level of organization
Some people need their work space to be very organized and neat. Others don't mind—and actually seem to prefer—a certain amount of clutter.

Noise
Some people like noise or music in the background while they work. Others require total silence.

Lighting
People have different needs. Some need bright lights; others prefer dimmer lighting. Some disabled readers have problems with fluorescent lighting but work well in natural light.

Temperature
Some people have difficulty concentrating if the room is too cold or too hot.

You probably can't control everything about the environment in which you tutor. However, you can try to be aware of the needs of the learner. You might also discuss these needs with the learner. Then the learner can consider them when planning where to study or do homework.

The Starting Point

Establishing Rapport and Building Trust

When you first meet the learner with whom you will work, one of the most important steps is to smile. A friendly greeting to establish rapport and to help the learner feel at ease is a good beginning. Listening to the learner tell you about himself or herself while getting acquainted is another important step. If the literacy program that you work with receives state and/or federal funds, you will be required to conduct a learner assessment. You can request information about the assessment from your program director. You will need to report information such as the learner's educational goals as well as his or her current skill level, as measured by a standardized test such as the Test of Adult Basic Education (TABE) or the Comprehensive Adult Student Assessment System (CASAS).

Initial Assessment

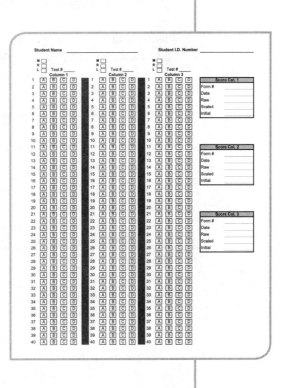

The initial learner assessment helps you to

- identify what the learner's goals and needs are, the abilities the learner already has, and the abilities he or she needs to develop

- plan instruction and identify teaching methods and materials most appropriate for the learner

- establish a baseline that can be used later to measure learner progress and ability to use literacy to meet personal needs

Suggestions for using assessment to measure a learner's progress during tutoring are discussed on pages 146–151.

There are four general types of initial assessment. Some literacy programs use a combination of types to meet different needs.

Standardized Tests

These tests are most like the standardized tests given in schools. They usually give results in terms of approximate grade-level equivalents. These results may not take into account an adult's knowledge and experience.

This statement illustrates the focus of standardized tests: "The results for the student indicate that he or she can read and write as well as the average student in grade _____."

Competency-Based Assessment

This kind of assessment measures a person's ability to apply basic skills in functional contexts, such as reading calendars, maps, traffic signs, and newspaper ads.

Competency-based assessment is best summed up with this sentence: "The student is able to use his or her reading and writing skills to perform the following functional tasks: _____."

Materials-Based Assessment

This form of testing helps determine where to place a learner in a specific set of instructional materials. It is rarely applicable to other materials.

This statement illustrates the focus of materials-based assessments: "The student has mastered the skills taught in the following materials: _____."

Performance Assessment

This form of assessment focuses on why the learner came to the program, what the learner wants to do with his or her new skills, and how the learner currently uses these skills in his or her own life. Performance assessment involves the learner in self-assessment. It helps the tutor understand what the learner thinks about reading, writing, or doing math and about being a learner. It involves the learner in a range of activities that can help expand his or her personal definition of literacy.

Performance assessment is summed up with this sentence: "The student has used his or her new skills (such as reading, writing, math) in the following ways: _____."

DOING YOUR OWN INITIAL ASSESSMENT

Some literacy programs may conduct an intake interview, do the initial learner assessment, and pass the information on to the tutor. In other programs, the tutor may need to do the assessment.

Activities 1–5, below, will help you learn more about the learner you will work with and be better able to design lessons to fit the learner's specific needs.

As you and the learner work through the assessment, you can make notes on a form like the one on pages 35–37. You may want to adapt the form and the activities to your own needs or program requirements. Both your observations and those of the learner are important in this process.

Activities 1–5 will help you work with a learner to explore the following five areas:

1. Background information (what experiences, responsibilities, and involvements the learner brings)

2. Current reading and writing (what the learner thinks about reading and writing and how the learner uses reading and writing now)

3. Reading and writing needs (what the learner wants to be able to do)

4. Abilities needed (what the learner needs to know in order to meet those needs)

5. Feelings about the assessment process

Don't try to cover all five areas in your first lesson. Gather the information informally during the first few meetings, giving the learner opportunities to demonstrate reading and writing abilities.

As you make your initial assessment, note any feelings that the learner has or observations that the learner makes about his or her strengths and weaknesses.

Activity 1

Background Information

Find out about these general areas:

*   Personal information—full name; address; phone numbers; best way to contact; age; physical needs related to hearing, sight, or mobility

*   Household—names and ages of children or grandchildren the learner is responsible for, other adults in the home

- Work—job the learner does now, name and address of employer, kinds of work the learner has done in the past

- Interests and hobbies—spare-time activities and what the learner likes about them

- Learning experiences as a child and teenager—name of school the learner attended and what school was like for him or her, last grade completed

- Learning experiences as an adult—classes in reading and writing, other kinds of classes (trade or technical, military, etc.), things the learner can do well and how he or she learned them, best learning experiences the learner has had as an adult and what made them good, adult learning experiences the learner liked least and why

SUGGESTION

You can list the things you'd like to know and then create a language experience story as the learner talks about them. (See Activity 7.)

Current Reading and Writing

ASK

- what the learner thinks makes someone a good reader or writer
- what the learner reads and writes now at home or at work, which of these tasks is easiest and why, and what is hard and why (what makes it hard)
- how the learner copes when he or she needs to read or write something and can't

Reading and Writing Needs

ASK

- how the learner thinks life would be different if he or she could read and write better
- why the learner decided to improve reading and writing now
- what reading and writing tasks the learner needs to be able to do to meet personal needs

- what reading and writing skills the learner needs to improve in order to do those tasks
- what the learner does when stuck on a word

Activity 4

Abilities Needed

Assess the learner's current abilities by using some of the techniques listed below. You do not have to follow this order. Stop if the learner seems frustrated or is clearly a beginner.

LISTENING COMPREHENSION

Read aloud to the learner an interesting passage that is appropriate for his or her knowledge and experience. Discuss the piece with the learner, and ask questions to check understanding.

SPEAKING

Have a conversation to get a sense of the learner's ability to express thoughts and feelings orally.

READING

Understanding

Show the learner several reading selections written at different levels. Then ask the learner to select one and try reading it. Afterward, ask the learner to explain what the selection was about. Ask how he or she felt about the level of difficulty and why. Ask if he or she wants to try any other selection. If the learner seems to have difficulty talking about the reading, ask him or her to read it aloud. Note the kinds of problems the learner has.

Point to numerals and letters on a chart, and ask the names (see page 107).

Oral reading

Use a text the learner has had success with. As the learner reads it aloud, make notes about fluency, ability to keep the place, use of punctuation cues, and expression. Also note if the learner consistently makes errors that might interfere with understanding, such as guessing words based only on the initial consonant sound or mixing up sounds for certain letters, and whether the learner self-corrects when an error is made.

Ability to use phonics
Check phonics knowledge in one of these ways:

1. Ask the learner to dictate a story or experience to you. Point to individual letters, digraphs, or consonant blends. Ask the learner first to read the word and then to give the sound of the letters.

2. Write the alphabet, digraphs, and some sample consonant blends. Ask the learner for the sound of each.

3. Write some made-up words, such as *shup* or *booch*, and ask the learner to sound them out.

4. Ask the learner to read aloud, and make notes of any errors or patterns of errors that emerge.

WRITING

Free writing
Ask the learner to write two to four sentences about some topic of interest. If necessary, suggest a topic related to his or her life. Ask the learner to guess at the spelling of any words he or she doesn't know for sure. Then ask the learner to read the piece aloud to you. Evaluate the legibility, spelling, punctuation, grammar, organization, and content.

Numerals and lowercase and uppercase letters
Say letters and numbers, one at a time, and ask the learner to print them on lined paper.

Cursive writing
Ask the learner to write his or her name in cursive writing.

Name, address, and phone number
Ask the learner to write his or her own name, address, and phone number.

Activity
5

Feelings About the Assessment Process

Ask how the learner feels about the assessment process. Find out if the learner's feelings about his or her reading and writing abilities have changed as a result of completing these tasks. Ask if the learner was surprised about anything.

Initial Assessment Form

Date _____

PART 1: BACKGROUND INFORMATION

Learner's Name _____   Age _____

Address _____

Telephone   Home/Cell _____   Work _____

Contact Information _____

Special Needs _____

Household/Family:

Work Experience:

Interests/Hobbies:

Previous Learning Experiences:

PART 2: CURRENT READING AND WRITING

What the learner thinks good reading and writing are:

What the learner reads or writes now:

Strategies the learner uses when faced with difficult tasks:

PART 3: READING AND WRITING NEEDS

Reasons the learner wants to improve reading and writing:

Things the learner needs to read and write:

Things about reading and writing the learner would like to improve:

PART 4: CURRENT ABILITIES *(include observations by both tutor and learner)*

Listening Comprehension

Strengths:

Needs:

Speaking

Strengths:

Needs:

Reading

Strengths:

Needs:

Writing

Strengths:

Needs:

PART 5: FEELINGS ABOUT THE ASSESSMENT PROCESS

Setting Goals

Goal setting is the cornerstone of learner-centered instruction. Many of your decisions about which methods and materials to use should depend on the learner's goals. Goal setting helps both you and the learner build a framework for planning and organizing lessons and monitoring progress. As you work together, you can revisit these goals and decide when they have been met, if they need to be modified, or if new ones need to be added. Goal setting increases motivation; and when people take small steps toward a goal, they often find that their motivation increases.

The information you obtain during the initial assessment will help you and the learner set beginning goals. If the learner finds it difficult to identify goals, it might help to review together some goals other learners have had. (See Appendix A.)

When a learner identifies a long-term goal, such as getting a good job or earning a GED credential, you will need to work together to break it into several short-term objectives. These objectives will allow the learner to see the path he or she will take to achieve the goal as well as to keep track of progress and remain motivated. You will then need to decide what activities will help the learner meet these objectives.

Be sure the activities you choose are realistic for the learner's skill level. In addition, be sure that they are concrete enough to assess so that the learner can see progress. The form on page 39 is an example of how a tutor worked with a student, Liz, to set short-term objectives and select instructional activities and materials to meet them.

Liz is a young mother with two children, ages three and five. She dropped out of school in the ninth grade and now works evenings as an aide in a local nursing home. Although she has some sight vocabulary, she is a poor reader.

My Goals

Long-range goal: <u>Be able to use a checking account to pay bills</u>

Short-term objective 1: <u>Be able to read bills, locate the amount owed,</u>
<u>and determine whom the check should be made payable to</u>

Activities	Methods/Materials
1. Learn to recognize by sight the words: due, payable, amount, owed, balance.	1. flashcards, sentences with these words missing—learner fills in the correct word
2. Circle the payee and amount owed.	2. learner's bills, copies of other bills

Short-term objective 2: <u>Be able to recognize and write number words</u>
<u>to one hundred</u>

Activities	Methods/Materials
1. Create reference chart with numerals and matching words to keep in purse.	1. index cards
2. Read number words in meaningful context.	2. language experience story about bills paid last month
3. Match number words to numerals.	3. reference chart, index cards with word or numeral on each

Ongoing Assessment

Observing and Recording Vocabulary Needs

As you work with the learner, continually observing learner progress and needs is key to supporting your lesson planning and instruction. For example, a learner reads a passage about political parties and doesn't understand it. After reviewing the passage with him, sentence by sentence, the tutor realizes that the learner misunderstood the meaning of the word *party* in this context. The learner thought it meant a fun get-together, because he only knows one definition for the word *party*. After explaining to the learner that the word *party* in this context means an organization or group, the reading passage makes sense to him.

Sometimes vocabulary terms that seem simple to a good reader may be confusing to a new reader, especially words that have multiple meanings. As a tutor, you will need to watch out for the context of the passages your learners read. You may need to pre-teach difficult vocabulary words before reading a passage. Keep track of words that your learner finds difficult. You may want to record them in a notebook so that you can review them again in upcoming lessons to support the learner's recall and memory of vocabulary. By continually observing, recording, and responding to the learner's needs, you will help his or her vocabulary grow.

Choosing Materials

You've probably noticed that any job is easier if you have the right tools. That's true of tutoring too. A good match between the learner and the materials improves communicating and learning.

Types of Materials

There are four general types of materials, and tutors and learners should work together to select those that best meet their needs. Examples of each are listed below. Books mentioned by title are published by New Readers Press and can be ordered online at http://www.newreaderspress.com or by phone at 800-894-2100.

PUBLISHED TEACHING MATERIALS

- To teach specific reading and writing skills: Choose a core reading and writing series that includes levels appropriate for your students, such as *Laubach Way to Reading* (levels 0–4), *Voyager* and *Endeavor* (levels 5–8), or *Challenger* (levels 1–8).

- To meet the information needs and interests of adult and young adult new readers: Choose engaging nonfiction materials at appropriate levels, such as *News for You* (weekly print or online newspaper with stories at levels 3–6), or *American Lives* (biographies of influential Americans at levels 3–4.5, 5–6.5, 6.5–8).

LEARNER-WRITTEN MATERIALS

- Language experience stories or free writing done as a class assignment

- New reader stories published by local literacy programs

REAL-WORLD MATERIALS

Examples of household and family-related materials include labels, magazines, newspapers, cookbooks, menus, children's storybooks, manuals, television listings, application forms, the Bible, forms from children's schools, medical history forms, and insurance forms.

Examples of work-related materials include memos and emails, orientation materials, manufacturer safety data sheets, charts and graphs, instructions, inventory sheets, procedure manuals, equipment instructions, and personnel policies.

TUTOR-PRODUCED MATERIALS

Examples of materials tutors can create to meet learners' needs include simplified information pieces, crossword puzzles, word games, flashcards, and family trees.

Most tutors find that using a combination of different materials often works best. If a learner is using a core reading series for primary instruction, you may want to supplement that series with other books or activities. Choose material that addresses the learner's goals or suits the learner's current situation. For example, if one of the learner's goals is to get a promotion, he or she may ask for help reading and filling out forms needed in the new job (real-world materials). Ask the learner to dictate a description of the job and turn that into a language experience story (learner-written materials). Then you can use both sample forms and the learner's own words to reinforce the reading skills taught in the core series.

Evaluating Materials

Early in the tutoring process, you may have to select some of the materials yourself. Check with your local library or literacy program to find out what materials they make available. As you get to know the learner and observe his or her successes, you will get better at selecting appropriate materials. As soon as possible in the tutoring process, involve the learner in selecting and evaluating materials.

In selecting materials, consider

- your purpose (e.g., to teach a specific reading or writing skill, to give information, or to provide a pleasurable experience)

- ways the materials will be used (e.g., independently or with tutor assistance)

- learner's background knowledge (Learners with extensive knowledge of a topic will be more likely to be able to read something somewhat above their current reading levels.)

- readability of the materials

The term *readability* refers to the qualities that make a reading selection easier or harder for a specific individual. In evaluating readability, you should look at both the physical format and the content of the materials. How many of the words will the learner recognize? Difficulty levels of the reading passages can be grouped according to ratios of known and unknown words. The reading material may frustrate the learners if they can read no more than 80–90 percent of the words without difficulty. The reading material may be instructionally appropriate if the learners can read more than 90 percent of the words, and the learners can read the material independently when they know closer to 100 percent of the words.

No materials will meet all criteria. You will have to decide which are most important and be prepared to compensate for difficulties. For example:

- If the learner wants to read the material but is missing some important background information or skills, you can help by discussing in advance what else the learner needs to know.

- If the material includes biased information or promotes stereotypes, you can identify these sections with the learner and discuss how the author's feelings or experiences might have influenced the author's point of view.

- If the type is too small, you can enlarge the page on a photocopier, use a bar that magnifies each line, or obtain an electronic copy that you can enlarge on a computer screen.

- If the material is designed to teach specific reading skills but does not provide enough practice, you can develop additional exercises.

Using Readability Formulas

Readability formulas are an objective tool to use in evaluating the difficulty of specific material. Readability formulas give results in terms of approximate grade levels. You should not make decisions solely on the basis of grade levels, especially when working with adults. However, this information, considered along with the other criteria listed in Appendix B, can help you make initial decisions about what materials might be appropriate.

There are many readability formulas. The word processing software on your computer may have a readability formula program built in. Readability levels may vary a bit from one formula to another. The best way to avoid this is to use the same formula for all materials and become familiar with how it rates each text.

Readability formulas are based on

- sentence length (A sentence is defined as any string of words that begins with a capital letter and ends with a period, exclamation mark, or question mark.)

- difficulty of the vocabulary or number of complex multisyllabic words

Keep the following in mind when you use a readability formula:

- Formulas give only an approximate grade level.

- The grade level may differ within the material, so choose three samples—one from near the beginning, one from the middle, and one from near the end.

- Do not automatically reject materials that seem too difficult based on a formula. A learner with high need or interest may be able and willing to read more difficult material.

- The best judge of the materials will ultimately be the learner.

Using the Fry Readability Graph

PURPOSE

To determine the reading level of written materials. (Some evaluators believe that the Fry Readability Graph is somewhat more accurate with materials written below the sixth-grade level.)

How	Example
1. Count three samples of exactly 100 words, one sample each from near the beginning, near the middle, and near the end of the selection. Do not count proper names or numerals. Count around them.	9.2 11.5 + 12.0 ————— 32.7
2. For each sample, count the number of sentences, estimating to the nearest tenth of a sentence.	
3. Add together the number of sentences in the three samples. Divide by 3 to get the average number of sentences per 100 words.	10.9 3)32.7
4. Count the number of syllables in each 100-word sample. (Do not count proper names and numerals. Count *-ed* as a syllable even if it is not pronounced separately, e.g., *helped*.)	109 120 + 115 ————— 344
5. Add together the number of syllables in all three samples. Divide by 3 for the average number of syllables per 100 words.	114.7 3)344
6. Plot the average number of sentences and average number of syllables on the Fry Readability Graph below. Most points should fall within the heavy lines that mark off the grade levels. If the plot falls in a gray area, the grade-level scores are not valid.	(second-grade level)

44

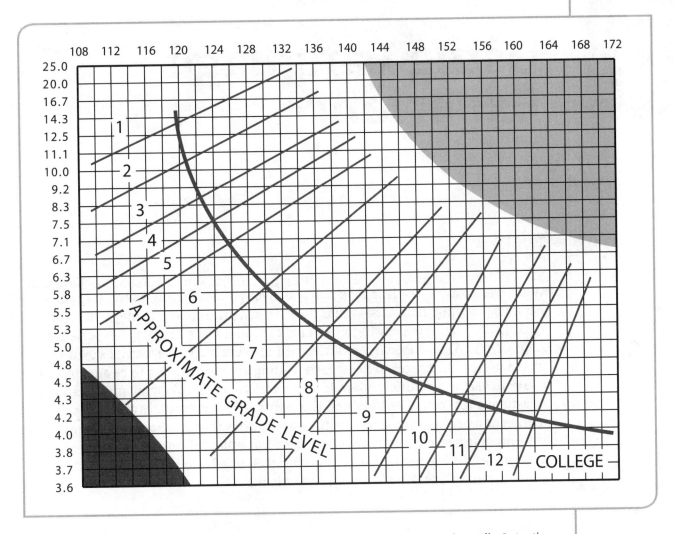

(Adapted from Edward B. Fry, "Readability Formula That Saves Time," Appendix 11-B in *Reading Instruction for Classroom and Clinic*, McGraw-Hill Book Co., 1972.)

6

Using Language Experience

Whenever possible, the learner should be involved in selecting or creating his or her own teaching materials, even if the involvement is only copying sentences, making flashcards, or creating a personal dictionary. The Language Experience Approach (LEA) described in Activities 7–13 involves using the learner's own words to create passages to help teach reading and writing. It can be adapted for use with learners at different levels. It can also be used with small groups and in one-to-one tutoring. LEA builds on the learner's life experiences and treats the learner as a person with ideas, feelings, and stories that are worth communicating. It incorporates the learner's own language. It is especially effective because it encourages the learner to use all four language acquisition and communication skills: listening, speaking, reading, and writing.

Activity 7

Creating a Language Experience Story

PURPOSE

To show the learner how his or her experience and speaking ability link to the written word even when the learner has little or no writing ability.

METHOD

Discuss

1. Ask the learner to tell a story about an experience.

Dictate

2. Print exactly what the learner says.

   Use correct spelling and punctuation, but do not change any words. Leave a blank line between each printed line in case you must make changes. For beginning readers, you don't need to write the whole story—three to five sentences is long enough.

3. Ask the learner to suggest a title for the story.

Verify

4. Read the story back to the learner, and ask for any corrections or changes.

Read

5. Read each sentence aloud, tracking the words with your finger, while the learner watches and listens.

6. Ask the learner to read each sentence after you.

7. Ask the learner to read the entire story.

File the story

8. Review the story at the next session. Type it, if possible, and print one copy for you and one for the learner. Place your copy in a binder or folder as part of a permanent collection of the learner's writing.

Activity 8

Generating Story Ideas

PURPOSE

To generate conversations that can be used as the basis of a language experience activity.

METHOD

1. Select one of the following ideas, or ask a question of your own.

What is your favorite hobby? Describe it.

If you could have three wishes, what would they be?

What type of work do you do? What do you like and dislike about your work?

What is the strangest thing that ever happened to you?

Tell me a story about someone in your family.

If you had as much time and money as you needed, how would you spend your vacation?

What is something you do well? How would you tell someone else how to do it?

What was the best choice you made in the last five years?

What do you most like to do on your day off?

Do you have a favorite song? Can you tell me the words?

Tell me about your favorite television show.

What would you say to the president if you met him or her?

Think about someone you know. Describe what he or she looks like.

2. Use the question to start a conversation with the learner.

3. When the learner is comfortable, ask the learner to repeat an interesting piece of information so you can write it down.

SUGGESTION

You can also work with the learner to create a map of ideas about a particular topic. (See Activity 75.) The learner can then choose one idea to use as the basis of an LEA story or can use one map for several different stories. Maps can also help generate new ideas and topics.

Activity

9

Videos, Pictures, and Photos as Story Starters

PURPOSE

To use videos, pictures, or photos to generate conversations that can be used as the basis of a language experience activity.

METHOD

1. Use a short video clip related to the learner's interests to start a conversation.

48

2. Bring a picture to the lesson, and ask the learner to describe it or ask how the learner feels about it.

3. Ask the learner to bring a personal photo to the lesson and tell you what is happening in the photo.

Newspaper and Magazine Articles as Story Starters

PURPOSE

To use timely or topical articles to generate conversations that can be used as the basis of a language experience activity.

METHOD

1. Read an article from a newspaper, magazine, or website to the learner. Then ask the learner to tell you about it in his or her own words.

2. Read a letter from a personal advice column, and ask the learner how he or she would answer it.

Using LEA with Beginning Readers

PURPOSE

To involve beginning readers in LEA activities without overwhelming them with the length or difficulty of the pieces.

METHOD

1. Follow the steps for obtaining an LEA story in Activity 7.

2. Keep the selection short—only one or two sentences.

3. Read the selection aloud together (see Activity 15) before the learner tries to read it alone.

SUGGESTIONS

- Write one of the following sentence starters, and ask the learner to complete it. Write as the learner dictates.

```
I want _____

I can _____

My children are _____

I wish _____

I like to go to _____

My best friend is _____

When I think of my mother, I _____
```

- Ask the learner to dictate a short list (e.g., names of family members, favorite foods, or places he or she would like to visit).

Activity 12
Using LEA with Groups

PURPOSE

To create a group language experience activity for a small group or class.

METHOD

1. Ask the group to select and discuss a topic. Then create a story on the board by asking each learner to contribute one sentence.

2. Write a sentence starter on the board. Then ask each learner how he or she would complete it. Write each learner's sentence on the board.

Activity 13
Building Skills with LEA Stories

PURPOSE

To use LEA to build a variety of skills.

METHOD

You can use LEA stories to teach many different skills. The learner is more likely to learn a skill that is connected to his or her own words. Work with the learner to choose what skill to work on. This encourages the learner to take responsibility for directing the learning. The learner can, for example:

- circle every *e* (or some other letter) in the story

- underline every capital letter

- count the number of sentences

- make flashcards for words he or she would like to learn (Ask the learner to practice until he or she can read the words by sight.)

- reconstruct one of the sentences using flashcards on which you have written each word

- make as many words as possible by changing the initial consonant sound in one of the words in the story (e.g., *went: bent, dent, lent*) (see Activity 27.)

- select words to have as sight words (You can help the learner with these words using the steps in Activity 19.)

- practice reading any direct quotes in the story—read them with appropriate emotion, such as excitement, anger, sadness, boredom, etc.

- name words that begin with the same consonant blend as a word in the story (e.g., *start: stop, stuck*) (You can write them down as the learner says them and then ask the learner to practice reading them.)

- select a word ending that the learner has already studied (such as *-s* or *-ing*), practice adding it to different words from the story, and then use each new word in a sentence (The learner can do a similar exercise by deleting endings from words in the story.)

- select a word with a long vowel sound and tell you what the word would be if the sound were changed to a short vowel (e.g., *made/mad*) (You could also reverse the process, e.g., *not/note*.)

- write contractions from the story and tell you what words they stand for (e.g., *wasn't/was not*)

- circle all the adjectives

- give a word or phrase that means the opposite of words you underlined in the story (e.g., *tall/short, got married/got divorced*)

- locate on a map the places mentioned in the story

- develop a list of words to learn to spell

- identify cause-and-effect relationships ("Why did this happen?")

- reread the story for fluency

Note: Many of the ideas in the other activities in this book can also be used with LEA stories.

7 Developing Fluent Reading

Many beginning readers who are unsure of themselves or are used to focusing on only one word at a time because of difficulties with decoding may read haltingly with little or no expression. They often pause and wait for the tutor to tell them how they're doing. They may read word by word instead of in fluent phrases. They need to develop confidence and learn to read fluently because fluent reading will improve their ability to understand and enjoy what they read. In addition, some learners have a specific goal that requires oral reading, such as reading stories to children or reading religious texts aloud.

What is fluent reading? John Kruidenier, Ed.D., stated in *Research-Based Principles for Adult Basic Education Reading Instruction* (The Partnership for Reading, 2002) that reading fluency refers to the speed and ease with which we read. When you think of reading fluency, consider three components:

- Reading speed

- Ease and comfort

- Expressiveness

Fluency is important for several reasons. First of all, it can increase reading comprehension. For example, a learner may understand the meaning of individual words but read too slowly to connect their meaning together. Or learners may read so slowly that by the time they reach the end of a sentence, they've forgotten what the beginning of the sentence was about.

The five reading techniques listed below are described in Activities 14–18. The one in Activity 14 provides the most support for the learner: The learner listens as you read aloud. The techniques in Activities 15–17 increase learner independence with the goal of moving to reading fluently. Rereading a sentence several times supports the development of fluency.

Reading Technique	Description
Reading aloud	Learner listens as tutor reads.
Duet reading	Tutor and learner read together.
Echo reading	Tutor reads and learner repeats.
Alternate reading	Tutor and learner read alternate sentences or paragraphs.
Phrasing with pencil tracking	Tutor models activity, and learner reads phrases aloud while using a pencil to connect the words in a phrase

Activity 14

Reading Aloud to the Learner

PURPOSES

- To allow the learner to hear someone read with good expression and phrasing modeling fluent reading.

- To enable the learner to benefit from (e.g., to gain information or enjoyment from) materials that are too hard to read independently.

- To provide a change of pace in the lesson.

- To enable you to share materials that are of personal interest, thus exposing the learner to new ideas and building the tutor-learner relationship.

METHOD

1. You read aloud to the learner.

2. The learner either follows along in a copy of the material or sits next to you and looks at your book while you read.

SUGGESTIONS

- You may use materials at any reading level.

- It is more important for the learner to hear you read than to follow along word by word in the book. If the learner becomes frustrated over losing his or her place while trying to follow along, ask the learner simply to listen.

Activity 15

Duet Reading

PURPOSES

- To give practice in fluent reading without putting the learner on the spot to read difficult material alone.

- To help the new reader learn to

  ▷ pay attention to punctuation marks

  ▷ develop good eye movement in order to keep his or her place

  ▷ read words in natural phrases

  ▷ increase the number of sight words

  ▷ read with expression

  ▷ read for enjoyment

METHOD

Use duet reading after the learner develops some basic sight vocabulary.

1. Choose something a little too hard for the learner. Help the learner select something that is somewhat above his or her current independent reading level. The material should be on a topic of interest to the learner. It may be a book, magazine or newspaper article, pamphlet, or brochure.

2. Begin reading together. Sit next to the learner, and read aloud together from the same selection. Read at a normal speed, using expression and observing punctuation. The learner reads along, trying to keep up with you.

3. Use your finger. Move your finger beneath the line as you read to help the learner keep up.

4. Keep going. Continue to read at a normal rate even if the learner hesitates or falls behind. Stop if the learner stops reading completely.

5. Don't ask questions. Do not stop to explain the meaning of a word unless the learner asks. Do not ask any questions to check the learner's comprehension because this material is to be used only as an oral reading exercise.

6. Decide if the reading material is too hard or too easy. If the learner keeps up easily, select more challenging material. If the material seems too difficult, use something that may be easier because it is written more simply or because the learner knows more about the subject.

SUGGESTIONS

- Use duet reading only for brief periods (7 to 10 minutes).

- Don't ask the learner to read aloud from the material alone because it is above the learner's independent reading level, which could be a frustrating experience.

- If you use duet reading at the beginning of a lesson, reread part of the same selection with the learner before the end of the lesson. Then the learner can see how much easier it gets with practice.

- Use this technique with the learner's own writing or with stories at the learner's level to practice fluent reading.

Echo Reading

PURPOSE

To provide support by modeling the reading before asking the learner to read it aloud independently.

METHOD

1. Select material that is somewhat above the learner's independent reading level.

2. For a beginning reader, read each sentence aloud, and then ask the learner to read it aloud. For a more advanced reader, model each paragraph instead of each sentence.

3. Encourage the learner to try reading independently as soon as he or she is comfortable doing so.

SUGGESTIONS

- After you both have read several sentences (or paragraphs), you might ask the learner to read the entire section again.

- You can also use this strategy with material at the learner's reading level if the learner needs help reading fluently.

- You can make recordings of the reading selections so the learner can practice reading aloud at home. You can also use audio e-books, available for free or for purchase online, or books with read-along recordings, available from various publishers. Also, many public libraries offer free audiobooks for download.

Activity 17

Alternate Reading

PURPOSE

To provide an opportunity for the learner to read aloud independently while also giving the learner breaks to relax and listen as someone else reads.

METHOD

1. Use materials that are at or slightly below the learner's independent reading level.

2. Read aloud one sentence (for beginning readers) or a paragraph (for more advanced readers).

3. Ask the learner to read the next sentence or paragraph aloud.

4. Repeat this process until you finish the passage.

SUGGESTIONS

- You may want to prepare the learner by first using either duet (Activity 15) or echo (Activity 16) reading on the same passage.

- Alternate reading works very well with plays or other materials with a lot of dialogue. If you use these types of materials, you might ask the learner to read only the part of a selected character.

- If you are working with more than one learner, you can divide the group into pairs and have them do alternate reading with each other.

Activity 18

Phrasing with Pencil Tracking

PURPOSE

To increase reading fluency using a multisensory technique to demonstrate and practice phrasing. (This multisensory technique has been presented at Orton-Gillingham training workshops. Pencil tracking activities can be developed for any reading level.)

METHOD

1. Choose print material to design the pencil tracking activity, and make multiple copies for modeling and practice. Choose words that the learner can recognize.

2. Place dots in the text marking the natural breaks between phrases or groups of words. Keep prepositional phrases intact.

3. Explain the activity to the learner, and model it.

4. Ask the learner to read aloud and swing a pencil from dot to dot. Provide feedback.

5. Repeat the activity.

6. Move the dots farther apart to lengthen the phrases, and repeat the activity.

Example:

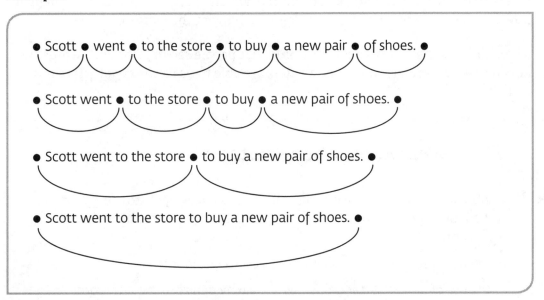

SUGGESTIONS

- You may design a pencil tracking activity using commercial text, student text, or other original text.

- Sentences may vary in length—combine short sentences and longer sentences. Activities can be one to several sentences in length.

- You can use words that are familiar to the learner to reinforce vocabulary and keep the focus on reading fluency.

- You can ask the learner to read the sentences aloud and to swing his or her pencil from dot to dot.

When students increase their reading fluency, usually their motivation increases as well. They see progress and can read with increased ease and enjoyment. Success motivates students to continue in instructional programs.

8 Recognizing Words: Alphabetics, Phonics, and Word Parts

To obtain meaning from text, a person must be able to understand the author's message and react to it using prior information and experience. This can't happen, however, if the reader is unable to recognize many of the words in the text.

Recognition is the ability to match words that people see in print with words they already use and understand. Good readers are able to use a variety of strategies to do this.

Word Recognition Strategies

Sight words   Words that readers recognize instantly without having to stop to figure them out. The more proficient readers are, the more words they recognize by sight.

Phonics   The use of sound-symbol relationships to decode words.

Word patterns   The use of familiar letter groupings to help recognize unfamiliar words or parts of words.

Context   The use of the surrounding words to help figure out an unfamiliar word.

Word parts   The use of root words, prefixes, suffixes, and other word parts to recognize a word.

No one strategy works for all situations, and readers sometimes use multiple strategies to figure out a word. So the more strategies a person learns, the more likely that person is to recognize words successfully. Activities 19–40 help teach these strategies.

The strategies can be taught in any order. Start by building on what the learner already knows.

Sight Words

PURPOSE

To help the learner recognize as many words as possible by sight in order to improve reading speed and comprehension.

METHOD

1. Work with the learner to choose the words he or she wants to learn.

    Examples:

    - Words that the learner uses often in daily life or words that are found in the learner's language experience stories

    - Words that appear often in print (high-frequency words), such as *the, there, this,* and *was*

    - Words with irregular spellings that are difficult to sound out phonetically, such as *height*

    - Everyday words and family names that appear on forms and applications, on job-related materials, on road signs, or in public places

2. Ask the learner to print the selected words on index cards. (You can help if needed.)

3. If the learner has trouble remembering the word, ask the learner to use it in a sentence. Write the sentence. Ask the learner to copy the sentence on the back of the flashcard. You can also ask the learner to draw a picture of the word on the back.

4. Ask the learner to look at each card and read it.

5. Encourage the learner to review the flashcards at home.

6. Review the words often.

SUGGESTIONS

- Teach no more than six to ten new words at a time. Use fewer cards if the learner has problems with that many.

- Periodically ask the learner to read the cards and divide them into two piles: those the learner knows and those he or she still has difficulty with. Work with the learner to reduce the size of the second pile.

- Play a game of Beat the Clock. Time how fast the learner can read the cards. Then challenge the learner to read them again and beat the previous time.

- Set a specific amount of time. Ask the learner to read as many cards as possible in that time. Repeat the exercise to show improvement.

- See Appendix C for a list of the 300 most frequently used words.

- See Appendix D for a list of social sight words that students may encounter in everyday life.

Activity 20

Phonics: Teaching Consonant Sounds

PURPOSE

To enable a learner to decode unfamiliar words by using knowledge of the sound-letter relationships.

METHOD

1. Select two or three words that begin with the same consonant and sound from the reading selection or the learner's language experience stories.

2. Ask the learner to write each word on a piece of paper and underline the initial consonant.

3. Ask the learner to name the letter. Teach it if necessary.

4. Say the sound of the letter, and ask the learner to repeat after you.

5. Ask for examples of other words that start with that sound, or give examples yourself.

6. Write these words on paper. Say the sound as you underline the letter at the beginning of the word. Be careful not to use words that start with the same letter but have different sounds. Examples: *park, phone.*

7. Have the learner practice identifying the sound in other words that are important in the learner's life.

8. If the learner has difficulty remembering a sound, ask the learner to choose a key word that will help. Examples: *car* for *c, hand* for *h.*

Activity 21
Phonics: Beginning, Middle, and End Sounds

PURPOSE

To enable a learner to recognize the same sound-letter relationship in various places in words.

METHOD

1. Select a sound that the learner now knows at the beginning of a sight word, a word he or she recognizes quickly.

2. Choose two additional sight words where the sound-letter is found in the middle of the word and at the end of the word.

3. Model for the learner the same sound at the beginning of a word, in the middle, and at the end of a word. An example is the sound /b/ in *ball, table,* and *cab.* Other words to use are *ball, basketball, rub* or *ball, rubble, rub.* Use words that are familiar to the learner. For example, the word *cabbage* may be familiar to one person but not another.

SUGGESTIONS

With each new sound or letter that the learner learns, continue to teach it at the beginning, middle, and end of words. As the learner practices the phonics patterns and applies them to new words, continue to provide the learner with practice reading the new sight words in sentences so that the learner begins to recognize the words.

- Use the same technique to teach consonant blends (*st, scr*) and digraphs (*sh*).

- After the learner can identify consonant sounds at the beginning of words, repeat the process to teach consonant sounds in the middle and at the end of words.

- Review sounds taught in previous lessons.

- For additional information on teaching phonics, see *Focus on Phonics, Patterns in Spelling, Laubach Way to Reading,* and *Challenger,* all published by New Readers Press.

- For assistance in teaching individual sounds, see Appendix E.

- To help you explain common phonics principles, see Appendix F. The rules are for your reference; you do not need to teach them unless you think that some might be helpful to the learner.

Phonics: Same or Different?

PURPOSE

To enable the learner to hear individual sounds in spoken words in order to improve decoding and spelling.

METHOD

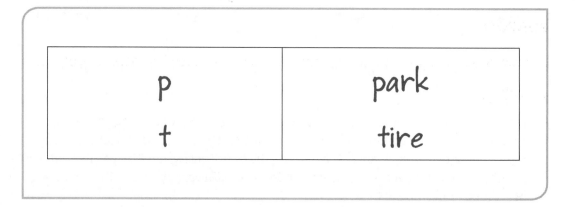

1. Select the initial consonant sounds you want to work on. List the letters in column 1.

2. In column 2, write a key word that begins with each letter. Select words from the reading selection or from the learner's language experience story.

3. Review with the learner the name and sound of each letter and the key word.

4. For each consonant, do the following:

   a. Say two other words that begin with this same consonant sound. Ask the learner if the first sound is the same or different for the two words.

   b. Ask the learner what letter each of the words begins with. Ask the learner to point to that letter in column 1.

   c. Say two other words: one that begins with this same sound, and one that does not. Ask the learner which one begins with the letter you are working on.

5. Repeat the process with other pairs of words (with same or different initial sounds) until you are sure the learner can hear the sound of the letter and distinguish it from other beginning sounds.

SUGGESTIONS

- Follow the same procedure with ending consonant sounds. Then work on digraphs and beginning and ending consonant blends.

- Adapt the procedure for use with vowel sounds.

Activity 23

Phonics: Bingo

PURPOSE

To provide a fun way to practice reading words that begin with consonant blends.

METHOD

1. Select the consonant blends you want to work on.

2. Divide two pieces of paper into squares like a bingo card (five columns across and five columns down). See the drawing on page 64 for an example.

3. On the first card, write a consonant blend in each of the spaces. (You can use some more than once.) Give this card to the learner.

4. Write the same blends on the second card, but put them in different places. Keep this card for yourself.

5. Select a word that starts with each blend you wrote. Write these 24 words on separate pieces of paper, and put them facedown in a pile.

6. Ask the learner to pick a word from the pile, read it aloud, and then give the sound of the blend.

7. Have him or her cover the matching blend on his or her own card with a square of blank paper or a coin. You should do the same.

8. The person who first covers five blends in a row (horizontally, vertically, or diagonally) wins and becomes the "caller" for the next game.

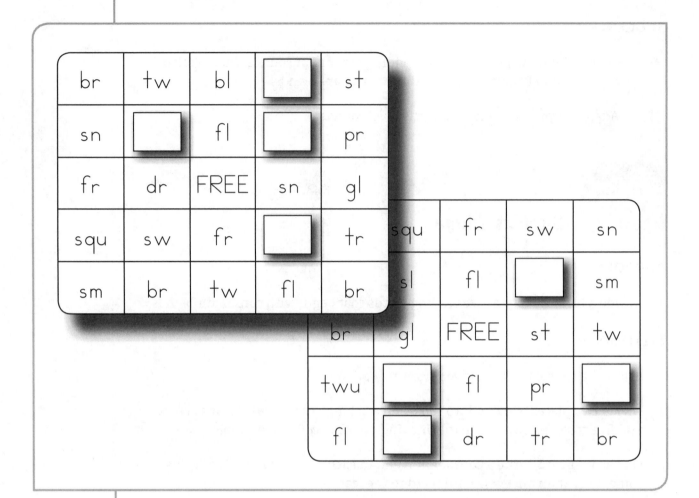

SUGGESTIONS

- This activity works well with a group.

- You can adapt the game by using words with ending consonant blends, digraphs, short vowels, *r*-controlled vowels, or any other phonic element the learner needs to practice.

Activity 24

Phonics: Start with the Vowel Sound

PURPOSE

To encourage more careful reading by a learner who tends to look only at the first letter in a word and then guess the rest of the word.

METHOD

1. Write the main vowel or vowel combination for a word. Below it, in a column, write the vowel or vowel combination, and add another letter or consonant blend. Continue to add letters in the column until you have the whole word at the bottom.

2. Cover all the letters in a word except the vowel at the top of the column. Say the vowel sound, and ask the learner to repeat it.

3. Uncover the letters in the following order, and ask the learner to add each new sound as you uncover it:

a	ou	a
ab	ous	ad
grab	hous	rad
	house	rade
		parade

Phonics: Decoding with Consonants

PURPOSE

To learn a way to decode a word when the learner is unsure of the correct vowel sound.

METHOD

1. If the learner comes to a word he or she can't read, ask the learner to underline each consonant and make the sound for each one.

2. Then ask the learner to blend the sounds together and try to figure out the word.

    Examples:

    <u>t</u>ur<u>tl</u>e   <u>c</u>a<u>b</u>i<u>n</u>e<u>t</u>

3. Ask the learner to read the sentence using that word and to check if it makes sense in context.

(Adapted from Mallory Clarke, *Goodwill Literacy Tutor Handbook*, Goodwill Literacy, 1991.)

Activity 26

Phonics: Teaching Syllables

PURPOSE

To enable learners to decode complex words by breaking words into syllables.

METHOD

1. Explain to the learner that a syllable is a word or part of a word that has only one vowel sound (not necessarily one vowel).

2. Give examples: *bat* (1), *head* (1), *pa/per* (2), *lit/tle* (2), *em/ploy/ment* (3).

3. Read words and ask how many vowel sounds the learner hears in each.

4. Teach the three rules listed below to a more advanced learner. (This is someone who is comfortable with the meaning of syllables and would benefit from more information about them.) Stop if the activity seems too difficult or frustrating for the learner.

5. Give the learner a list of words.

6. Ask the learner to put a dot under each vowel.

7. Ask the learner to cross out any final *e*'s.

8. Ask the learner to underline digraphs and consonant blends.

9. Ask the learner to divide the words according to the three rules.

10. Ask the learner to repeat the word, connecting the syllables and saying the whole word.

Three rules for syllables

1. The two-consonant rule:

   • If there are two consonants between the vowels, divide the word between the consonants.

in/to	les/son	traf/fic	fen/der

- Do not divide blends or digraphs.

bash/ful   em/blem

2. The one-consonant rule:

    - If the word has only one consonant sound between two vowels, divide the word before the consonant. If the vowel comes at the end of a syllable, it will usually have the long sound.

ba/con   fe/male

    - The letter *y* in the middle or at the end of a word acts as a vowel.

sy/phon   la/dy

3. The one-consonant "oops" rule:

    - Sometimes the one-consonant rule does not work. When that happens, divide the word after the consonant. The vowel will have a short sound.

lem/on   vis/it   sec/ond   ov/en   trav/el

SUGGESTION

To help the learner hear the number of syllables, tap your finger on the table as you say each syllable. Later, the learner can do that independently.

(Adapted from Ed Robson, Marsha DeVergilio, and Donna DeButts, LITSTART: *Literacy Strategies for Adult Reading Tutors*, Michigan Literacy, Inc., 1990.)

Word Patterns

PURPOSE

To help the learner recognize new words more quickly without having to sound out and blend each individual sound in the word.

METHOD

1. Make sure the learner understands the concept of rhyming. Say several pairs of words, and ask if they rhyme.

2. Then choose a word pattern with which you can create several rhyming words. Example: *-it.*

3. Write the word pattern at the top of a piece of paper, and ask the learner to say the sound. If the learner doesn't know, say it yourself. Example: *-it.*

4. Write a rhyming word under the word pattern. Example: *sit.* Ask the learner what the word is. If the learner doesn't know, read it yourself.

5. Write another rhyming word by changing the initial consonant. Example: *bit.* Ask the learner to read it. If the learner has difficulty, give a hint: "If *s-i-t* is *sit,* then what is *b-i-t?*"

6. Keep adding words and asking the learner to read them.

7. Ask the learner to add other words using the same pattern.

8. Ask the learner to read through the entire list.

   Example:

   -it
   sit
   bit
   fit
   hit
   lit
   flit

SUGGESTIONS

- Remember that this recognition strategy can also be helpful for figuring out multisyllabic words.

Example:

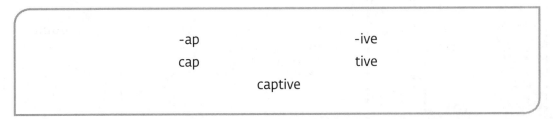

-ap   -ive
cap   tive
            captive

- Do not confuse a beginning learner by using ending sounds that can be spelled more than one way. Examples: *fix* and *picks*, *tax* and *stacks*.

- When the learner is comfortable with a pattern, dictate other words that have the same pattern, and ask the learner to write them.

- When the learner is reading and encounters an unfamiliar word, ask the learner to apply the word pattern he or she learned to help him or her sound out the word.

- See Appendix G for examples of common word patterns.

Activity 28

Word Patterns for Kinesthetic/Tactile Learners

PURPOSE

To involve the learner in physical activities that teach the concept of word patterns.

METHOD

Flashcards

1. Select the word endings you want to work on. Ask the learner to write each ending on a separate index card. Examples: *-ash, -act, -ack, -ent, -each.*

2. Make a list of each of the consonants, digraphs, and consonant blends you want to work with. Ask the learner to copy each of these on a separate index card.

3. Ask the learner to place one of the consonant cards in front of a word pattern card and read the new word. (Nonsense words are allowed. The emphasis is on

recognition, but you may want to discuss whether or not a new word is a real word.)

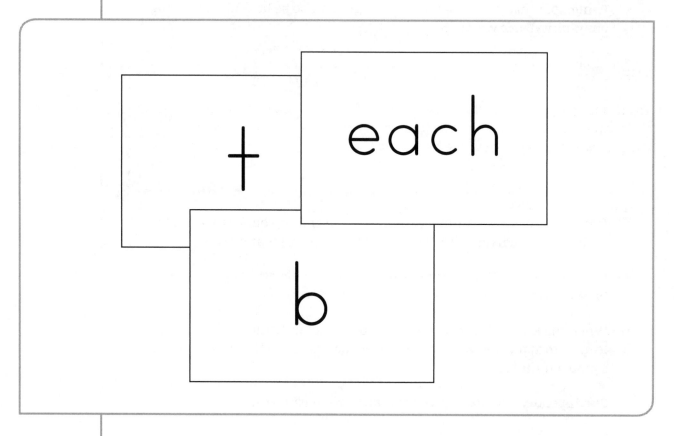

Concentration game

1. Select six pairs of words. Each pair should have the same ending pattern (one the learner has already studied). Examples: *snack/pack, dust/rust.*

2. Write each word on a separate index card.

3. Mix the cards up, and lay them facedown in three rows.

4. Ask the learner to turn over two cards at a time, trying to find the two words that have the same ending pattern. Ask the learner to read each word aloud, and if the patterns match, remove the cards from the game. If not, the learner should turn them facedown again.

5. Alternate turns (tutor and learner or two learners) until all the cards are gone.

SUGGESTION

You can also use this game to help the learner recognize words with and without the silent *e* pattern. Examples: *bit/bite, hop/hope.*

Activity 29

Context: Just Say "Blank"

PURPOSE

To encourage the learner who comes to an unfamiliar word to continue reading and then return to it later and use context information to figure it out. (This strategy is appropriate when the context of the sentence can help the reader make sense of the word, such as with nonfiction text that includes topic-specific vocabulary.)

METHOD

1. When the learner comes to a word he or she doesn't recognize, tell the learner to just say "blank" and keep reading.

2. Encourage the learner to use the rest of the sentence or paragraph to try to think of a word that would make sense (is logical, has meaning, and is grammatically appropriate) in place of the unknown word.

3. If there is more than one possibility, ask the learner to see if the first sound in the word helps narrow down the choices.

4. Ask the learner to read the sentence with the word selected to be sure it fits the context.

5. If the word fits the context but isn't the written word, then reinforce that the choice makes sense. Then read the written word aloud, and have the learner add it to his or her list of new vocabulary words. The new word can be reviewed again later during tutoring.

Activity 30

Context: Cloze Exercise

PURPOSE

To help the learner practice using context—the meaning of surrounding words and sentences—to identify unknown words in a sentence or paragraph by filling in missing words from a text. (The word *cloze* comes from *closure* and means finishing or "closing" a sentence.)

METHOD

1. Make a cloze exercise by selecting a passage that is at or below the learner's current reading level. Leave the first sentence intact, and then delete words in the subsequent sentences. Select words for which there are context clues that can be used to identify the missing words. Example: "There were four eggs in the bird's _____," not "There were _____ eggs in the bird's nest."

2. Ask the learner to fill in the missing words.

SUGGESTIONS

- Remind the learner that it is most important to choose words that make sense in context. Unless the learner is working from a word list, it is not important to fill in the exact word.

- See Activity 59 for suggested cloze activities to teach writing.

Activity 31

Context: Using Cloze with a Beginning Reader

PURPOSE

To provide additional support to help the beginning reader successfully complete cloze exercises.

SUGGESTIONS

- Keep the passage short.

- Delete very few words and no more than one per sentence.

- If necessary, provide a word list for the learner to choose from.

- Use material with which the learner is already familiar, such as a language experience story or a passage from a previous lesson.

- If the material is new, give the learner an overview of the contents before he or she starts reading.

- Delete only one kind of word, such as nouns, in each passage. Tell the learner what kind of word you deleted.

- Provide a choice of two words for each blank. You can also write the first letter of the word in the blank space so that the learner has both context and phonics clues.

- Provide the exact number of spaces for the letters in the deleted word.

- Ask the learner to say the missing word rather than write it.

- Ask the learner to explain why the word he or she chose seems to be a good fit.

Activity 32
Word Parts: Compound Words

PURPOSE

To help the learner put words together to form compound words.

METHOD

1. Select five or six compound words that are made up of smaller words that the learner can already read.

2. Put the first half of each word in one column.

3. Put the second half of each word in a second column.

4. Ask the learner to connect the two words that form a compound word and then read the new word.

5. If you're not sure that the learner recognizes the word, ask the learner to use it in a sentence.

   Example:

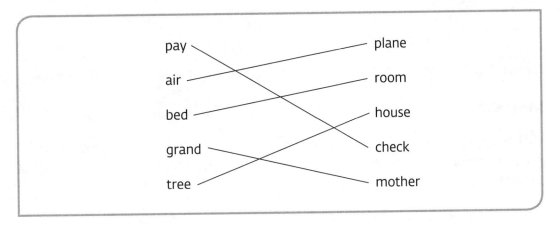

SUGGESTIONS

- Use drawings or pictures of two words to show the meanings of the separate words and the meaning of the compound word they make.

  Example:

tree + house   = treehouse

- See Appendix H for a list of common compound words.

Activity 33

Word Parts: Distinguishing Between Plural and Possessive Endings

PURPOSE

To help the learner distinguish between the plural and possessive noun endings.

METHOD

Use this method only after the learner has had a chance to read both plural and possessive words in context and has discussed how the endings affect the meaning of the word.

1. Make three columns on a paper.

2. In the first column, list five or six nouns that the learner already knows. Ask the learner to read them.

3. Write *s* at the top of the second column.

4. Write *'s* at the top of the third column.

5. Read a sentence using the plural or possessive form of the word in column 1.

6. Ask the learner to write the word under the correct column heading.

Example:

Ann is the boy's mother.

Noun	-s	's
boy		boy's
girl		
doctor		
cat		
mother		

SUGGESTION

You can adapt this activity to teach other word parts. Examples: *s/es, d/ed.*

Word Parts: Adding Endings to Words

PURPOSE

To help the learner select the correct rule when adding endings to words.

METHOD

1. Select the ending you will work on. Example: *-ing.*

2. Select the type of word to which you will add the ending. Example: verbs that end in *e.*

3. Explain to the learner the rule for adding the ending to this type of word. Example: When the word ends in *e,* drop the *e* before adding *-ing.*

4. Make two columns on a sheet of paper. In the first column, list four to six words that illustrate the rule you just taught.

    Example:

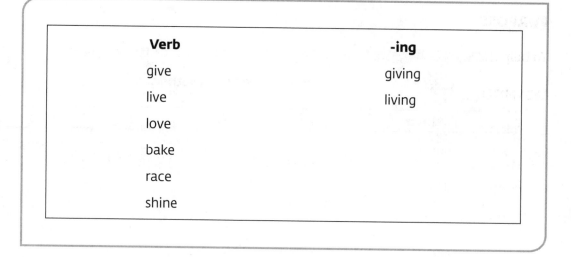

Verb	-ing
give	giving
live	living
love	
bake	
race	
shine	

5. Ask the learner to read the first word and tell you what the word would be if the ending were added. Then write that word in the second column, or ask the learner to write it.

6. Ask the learner to write the rest of the words.

7. Finally, ask the learner to say a sentence using the words in each column.

SUGGESTIONS

-   You can modify this activity to fit almost any word ending.

-   With a beginning reader, you can create a list where the learner applies the same rule to each word (as in the example above).

-   With a more advanced learner, you can mix the words. Ask the learner to decide which rule to use before adding the ending. Examples: *give, hit, kick.* Ask the learner to say the word with the ending *-ing* and then apply the correct rule to write the new word (*giving, hitting, kicking*).

-   See Appendix F for rules on adding endings.

Word Parts: Prefixes

PURPOSE

To help the learner recognize how adding a prefix changes the meaning of a word.

METHOD

1. Select the prefix you want to work on, and discuss its meaning.

2. Make a two-column chart. List words that begin with that prefix in the first column. Help the learner read them.

3. In the second column, write sentences using words the learner already knows. Leave a blank for the missing word.

4. Ask the learner to select the correct word from the first column to complete each sentence.

    Example:

unhappy	I left in a hurry with the beds _____.
uncomfortable	I found two _____ bills on the table.
unmade	She seemed _____ in the movie.
unpaid	The chair was hard and _____.
uninterested	He looked tired and _____.

SUGGESTION

See Appendix I for a list of prefixes and suffixes and their meanings.

Activity 36

Word Parts: Changing Root Words

PURPOSE

To help the learner understand how adding a prefix or suffix to a root word can change its meaning.

METHOD

1. Select five or six words that have both a prefix and a suffix.

2. Ask the learner to underline each prefix and circle each suffix.

    Examples:

    uninterested   nontraditional

3. Ask the learner to use the root word in a sentence. Write the sentence, or ask the learner to do it.

4. Ask the learner to use the root word with the prefix or suffix in a sentence. Write the sentence.

5. Ask the learner to use the word with both the prefix and the suffix in a sentence. Write the sentence.

6. Discuss how adding the prefix or suffix changed the meaning of the word.

7. Do the same for each word.

Activity 37

Word Parts: Contractions

PURPOSE

To help the learner recognize that a contraction is made up of two words.

METHOD

1. Write several sentences that use contractions.

2. Ask the learner to read each sentence and underline the contraction. (Read the sentences to the learner if he or she has trouble.)

3. Ask the learner to write the two words that make up the contraction next to each sentence.

   Examples:

   Her mother <u>isn't</u> going to say yes.   is not

   He <u>can't</u> get these until noon.   can not

Applying New Skills to Meet Everyday Needs

Good readers are able to apply information they learn from reading to help them meet their everyday needs. One of a tutor's major responsibilities is to design activities that help the learner build bridges between the tutoring sessions and the learner's daily life. Activities 38–40 help learners develop reading skills that can teach them to do this.

Activity 38

From Here to There

PURPOSE

To give the learner practice in reading words related to giving directions: *right, left, straight, street, blocks, turn,* etc.

METHOD

1. With the learner, make a map of the learner's neighborhood. Include street names. (Before doing this, you might have to introduce the learner to the concept of maps and how they are used.)

2. Mark where the learner lives. Ask the learner to identify several other landmarks: grocery store, post office, factory, school, park, etc. Mark these on the map.

3. Write directions from the learner's home to one of the landmarks, but do not name the destination.

4. Ask the learner to follow the map while reading the directions and then identify the destination.

SUGGESTIONS

- Reverse roles and ask the learner to write the directions. (A beginning writer can dictate them to you.)

- When working in a group, divide learners into pairs. Ask everyone to write a note to their partner with directions to their home or to a landmark in the neighborhood.

Activity 39

Making a Grocery List

PURPOSE

To help the learner read the grocery ads in a newspaper and words related to food.

METHOD

1. Bring in or print out a local grocery ad or flyer.

2. From a page or two of the ad, make a shopping list of 10 to 12 of the advertised items.

3. Ask the learner to find the items in the ad and write the price on the list next to each item.

4. Ask the learner to add the prices and find out what the total bill will be. Provide help if needed.

SUGGESTIONS

- Reverse roles and ask the learner to make a grocery list for you from the ad.

- Cut food words out of the paper, or write a list of food words. Ask the learner to categorize them and show where in the store they can be found (e.g., meat department, dairy department, or produce department).

Activity 40

Building Bridges

PURPOSE

To help the learner see how information from the tutoring session can be applied to a variety of real-life activities.

SUGGESTIONS

- Bring in a movie schedule, and practice finding the theater and showtimes where a particular movie can be seen.

- Bring in a TV schedule, and find the time and channel of various programs.

- Read washing instructions on an item of clothing.

- Go to the store, and choose a greeting card for a friend's birthday.

- Read a bus schedule, and figure out what bus you would need to take to reach your destination by 3:00 p.m.

- Read cooking directions on a food package.

- Clip and use grocery coupons.

- Locate newspaper job ads of interest.

- Read the recommended dosages on an over-the-counter medication.

- Chart your family tree.

- Copy signs on your street. Practice reading them in class.

- Read about an interesting person or place.

- Practice reading a storybook so you can read it to your child.

- Read a letter to a columnist. Write or dictate your own answer. Compare your answer to what the columnist actually wrote.

- Learn a new game by reading the directions.

Activities on this list should be selected based on learner interest.

Building Vocabulary

You may use Activities 41–45 to help develop your learner's vocabulary. In addition to vocabulary words you will find in the texts you use with the learner, you may want to use these vocabulary lists included in the appendixes:

- Appendix J: Academic Vocabulary—terms and phrases that may be used in instructional materials

- Appendix K: Banking- and Work-Related Vocabulary—terms and phrases that may be used in banking and with money or in jobs or job seeking

- Appendix L: Health-Related Vocabulary—terms and phrases that may be used by health care workers, in medical situations, or with descriptions of illnesses

Building Vocabulary with Pictures, Symbols, and Graphics

PURPOSE

To help learners understand and remember new vocabulary words.

METHOD

1. Choose four to six new words that are contextually related. Examples: *doctor, hospital, medicine, temperature, health*. Choose words related to a context that is important to the learner such as work-related, health-related, family-related, money-related, or sports-related terms. Include some verbs in the new vocabulary.

2. Find pictures, symbols, or graphics that help the learner connect the words to a visual image.

TEACHING ADULTS: A LITERACY RESOURCE BOOK

3. Introduce the vocabulary words, one at a time, using the visual cues.

4. Say the word, show the word in print form, and use the word in a sentence.

5. Ask the learner to use the word in a sentence.

6. Ask the learner to write the word.

7. Ask the learner to write a sentence using the word.

8. Ask the learner to create a flashcard that will help him or her remember the meaning of the word. Have the learner write the word on one side of the card, and on the other side, have him or her put the meaning, a visual cue, other words similar to the word, or a sentence with the word.

9. Continue the process with the other vocabulary words.

10. Have a conversation using several of the words.

11. Practice using the words by reading text that uses some of the words.

Building Vocabulary with Word Capsules

PURPOSE

To teach unfamiliar vocabulary by grouping words around a single topic or theme in a "word capsule."

METHOD

1. List 8 to 12 important terms related to a single topic that the learner needs or wants to learn about. The list may include words from a text that the learner has to read or special sight words that the learner needs to know.

Examples:

Banking words	
deposit	teller
withdrawal	account
interest	balance
statement	loan

Car tune-up words	
carburetor	spark plugs
points	oil filter
timing	air filter
gap	idle

2. Write the list on the board or on paper.

3. Define each word and use it in context. If the words are also used in a text you are reading, point them out to the learner.

4. Ask the learner to use each word in a sentence.

SUGGESTIONS

- If you are working with a group of learners, have them pair up and take turns using the words in sentences. Then ask them to write their sentences and read the sentences aloud.

- If you are working with a beginning reader, create shorter word capsules. Ask the learner to dictate sentences using each word. Write the sentences on paper, and ask the learner to recopy them.

- Encourage learners to develop their own word capsules for topics they are interested in.

- Instead of asking more advanced readers to write separate unrelated sentences, ask them to write an entire paragraph or essay using the word capsules.

(Adapted from Mary Dunn Siedow, "Instructional Strategies" in *Teaching Adult Beginning Readers: To Reach Them My Hand*, Alan M. Frager [ed.], College Reading Association, Monograph Series, 1991.)

Activity 43
Building Vocabulary with Synonyms

PURPOSE

To help learners connect new words to words they already know to improve the recall and memory of new words.

METHOD

1. Choose four to six new words that are connected to a context to which the learner can relate, such as work, health, family, money, or sports. Include some verbs in the new vocabulary.

2. After choosing a word to teach (e.g., the word *conversation*), determine which synonyms the learner already knows related to the verb *converse* or its noun form *conversation*. The learner may know such words as *talk, chat, speak, discuss/discussion*.

3. Have the learner read the familiar words in a sentence, and then introduce the new word, *conversation*, as a noun.

4. Show the learner the word in writing, pronounce the word, define it, and then use it in a sentence.

5. Give the learner opportunities to practice using the new word, and review the word by connecting it to the familiar vocabulary. Provide opportunities for the learner to read and write the new vocabulary.

Building Vocabulary with Multiple Meanings

PURPOSE

To teach learners the breadth and depth of meanings of words so that they can improve their reading comprehension.

METHOD

1. Start with a common word like the word *cold*, and ask the learner what it means and to use it in a sentence, or have the learner read the word in a sentence and talk about the meaning.

2. Explain that many words have more than one meaning. Use *cold* as an example. Add a second meaning to the word *cold*. The two most common meanings of the word *cold* are "less warm" and "a common illness."

3. When the learner knows the most common meanings, introduce another meaning. Over time, you can help the learner understand and comprehend the depth of the meaning of the word. Other examples of how *cold* is used are *cold shoulder, cold war, cold cuts, cold fusion, cold personality, cold call, he nailed it cold, out in the cold, brought in from the cold, cold cream.*

4. Repeat the steps with more vocabulary words, starting with the most common meaning and then adding multiple meanings.

Building Vocabulary with Games

PURPOSE

To provide fun practice to help learners recall the meanings of words.

METHOD

1. Root words can be practiced in a matching game. List four root words that the learner has previously learned in one column. Write the matching meanings in a column to the right, in no particular order. Have learners match the root to the meaning.

    Example:

    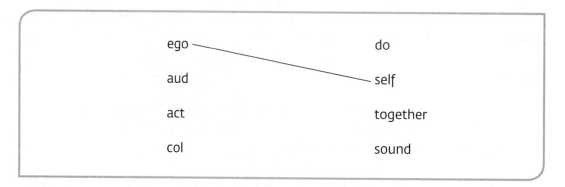

ego	do
aud	self
act	together
col	sound

    Provide words that are familiar to the learner that show how the roots are used, such as *auditory, collaborate* or *collide, action, egomania.*

2. Compound words can also be practiced in a matching game. List four compound words that the learner has previously learned.

    Example:

    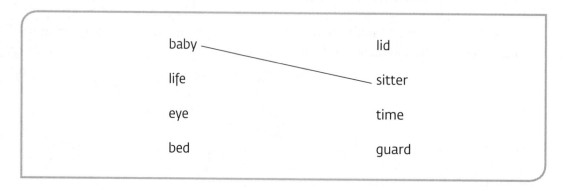

baby	lid
life	sitter
eye	time
bed	guard

    Have the learner match words to make compound words and then use each completed compound word in a sentence. In small groups, have teams design the activity for other teams. There are also many compound word games on the Internet that will provide additional practice for learners.

Developing Reading Comprehension

In order to make meaning from written material, effective readers should be able to do the following:

- Recognize: Match printed words with words for which they already know the meanings.

- Understand: Understand the intended message, both what the author says and what can be inferred from the text, and interpret information.

- React and respond: Compare and integrate the information in the text with their own knowledge and prior experiences, and evaluate the information to draw relevant conclusions.

- Apply: Use the new knowledge or skills gained from the reading to apply in other contexts or to meet personal needs.

Effective listeners also need to be able to do these same things.

Understanding and Reacting: Avoiding Comprehension Roadblocks

A learner who can recognize all the words in a passage is not necessarily able to understand the passage or react to it using personal knowledge and experience. Several roadblocks can interfere with even the most experienced reader's ability to understand and react to reading material.

As you work with a learner, try to anticipate when these roadblocks might occur. With careful planning, you can avoid some or teach the skills necessary to get beyond them. Activities 46–56 can help you do so.

Roadblocks to understanding and reacting might include the following:

- Lacking background information (example: reading an article about a political dispute in another country without knowing where the country is or any of the history leading up to the event)

- Reading unfamiliar vocabulary (example: reading words in directions for connecting a DVD player to a television that include technical terms, such as *coaxial cable, 75/300 ohm matching transformer*)

- Having difficulty changing initial assumptions when they are incorrect (example: starting to read a newspaper article titled "Running in Place" thinking it's about exercise and becoming confused when the article discusses staying in the same job for too long)

- Being unfamiliar with page layout (example: not knowing how to follow the columns in a newspaper or how to find a story that is continued on another page)

- Overlooking details or missing a key sentence (example: failing to read the *not* in this sentence: "She did not know the name of the man who called.")

- Getting lost in details and missing the main idea (example: getting caught up in the description of something that happened to a character and missing clues that the person is describing a dream, not something that is actually happening)

- Being unfamiliar with such graphic elements as diagrams, charts, or maps (example: not knowing how to read a diagram that shows how to hook up electronic equipment)

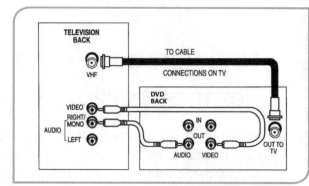

- Being unfamiliar with a typeface or handwriting (example: being unable to decipher someone's handwriting or read a fancy typeface)

- Being unfamiliar with the style of writing or genre (example: reading poetry or Elizabethan English for the first time)

Making Predictions

PURPOSE

To improve comprehension by actively engaging the learner in reading and making meaning from the text.

METHOD

1. Ask the learner to make predictions at the following points:

    •   Beginning of the reading ("Read the title. What do you think the story will be about?")

    •   During the reading ("Do you think Sue will decide to have a baby?")

    •   Before the end ("Who do you think the murderer was?")

2. Write the learner's predictions in a chart like the one below.

3. Ask the learner to compare the predictions to what the text says. "Was your prediction correct? Did what you predict happen?"

My prediction	Correct?	Incorrect? What really happened?	No evidence or not addressed?

SUGGESTION

Ask the learner to predict some of the words that might be used in the story (after reading the title, looking at any accompanying illustrations, and discussing the general content). In addition to aiding comprehension, this can help prepare the learner to recognize unfamiliar words in the text that may be a part of his or her speaking vocabulary but not reading vocabulary. After the learner reads the story, ask, "Did the author use those words? Why or why not?"

Before-During-After (Directed Reading)

PURPOSE

To introduce the learner to a process that readers can use to increase their understanding of written materials. (See Activity 48 for suggestions about how to help a learner begin to use this process independently.)

METHOD

Before the learner reads the selection, do the following:

1. Introduce and preview the reading selection. Ask the learner to look at the headline, title, or headings and predict what the piece will be about.

2. Discuss the topic, and find out what the learner already knows about it.

3. Help the learner identify a purpose for reading. For example, the learner could identify something to find out. Tutor says, "When you look at this title, what are you curious to find out from this reading?"

    Additional examples:

    > *Tutor:* "Please find out what happened when Bob was late for work."
    >
    > *Learner:* "I'd like to know why the mayor is against the Police Review Board."

During the reading, do the following:

4. Encourage the learner to make predictions about content and what will happen next, or check to see whether the learner's questions have been addressed yet.

5. Help the learner correct the predictions by comparing them to what the selection actually said to check understanding.

After you and the learner have finished reading a passage, do the following:

6. Discuss what the selection actually said (literal understanding).

7. Discuss what the reader had to figure out—the message between the lines (inferred understanding).

8. Identify what else the learner would like to know.

TEACHING ADULTS: A LITERACY RESOURCE BOOK

SUGGESTIONS

- Some learners may not be aware of what happens in a person's mind during reading. You can model this process by "thinking aloud" and sharing your thoughts as you read aloud to the learner.

- With a longer text, you can ask the learner to read a section at a time using the above steps. Place a mark at the end of each section to show the learner where to stop.

Activity 48

Creating Independent Readers

PURPOSE

To encourage the learner to begin to use the before-during-after strategy (Activity 47) outside of class to improve understanding while reading independently.

METHOD

Print questions on index cards (as shown below) for the learner to take home.

Before I Read

1. What is this going to be about?

2. What do I already know about this topic?

3. What's my purpose for reading this?

While I Read

4. What do I think the next part is going to be about?

5. Was I right or wrong?

6. What else do I want to know about this topic?

After I Read

7. What did the article tell me?

8. What did I have to figure out?

9. What else do I want to know about this topic?

SUGGESTION

The learner can practice this strategy even on materials he or she cannot read alone. By reading aloud to the learner, you can also introduce the learner to a variety of types and styles of writing while developing comprehension skills.

Activity 49

Asking Questions

PURPOSE

To help the learner go beyond literal understanding, infer meaning from the text, and add to the meaning by applying personal experiences or ideas.

METHOD

After each reading, ask at least one of each of the following types of questions.

Literal questions: What does the text say?

Examples:

> - Where did Sam go when he left the house?
> - How was Sandra's family different from Jackie's family?
> - What are the steps involved in making a quilt?

Inferential questions: What can be inferred from the text? ("What is written between the lines?")

These questions are not specifically answered in the text, but the reader can figure out the answers by using the literal information provided.

Examples:

> - What is the main idea of the reading?
> - Do you think Anne was a good mother? Why or why not?
> - Can you tell whether or not Bob liked his job? How?

Applied questions: What is the reader thinking?

Learners must draw on their own background knowledge, beliefs, and experiences to answer these kinds of questions.

Examples:

> - Was this an effective story or article? Why or why not?
> - Do you think Maria made a good decision when she decided to marry Al? Why or why not?
> - What would you have done if you were Jane?

SUGGESTIONS

- Try to ask questions that are related to each other. Your questions should lead the learner from literal understanding to a discussion of underlying ideas and how these ideas apply to his or her own experiences. For example, you could ask this series of questions: "According to the article, what are the steps involved in making a quilt? What would make a person a good quilter? Do you think you could be a good quilter? Why or why not?"

- Write two or three examples of each type of question for a reading the learner will do in class. Put each question on a separate index card or piece of paper. Place the questions upside down in three piles. Ask the learner to select and answer questions from each pile.

- Have the learner answer the questions orally or in writing depending on his or her skill level.

- If you are working with a group, ask each person to make up a question for the others to answer.

Activity 50

Tell Me What You've Read

PURPOSE

To allow the learner to demonstrate understanding by describing and summarizing a reading passage to a partner.

METHOD

1. Choose two reading passages written at the learner's independent reading level.

2. Read one passage to yourself while the learner reads the other one silently.

3. After this silent reading, have the learner describe the contents of his or her article to you; then you do the same.

4. Exchange passages and read the second passage silently.

5. Share your ideas about what you both read.

Note: Partners can also discuss how hearing someone talk about the passage before they read it helped them get more from their own reading of the passage.

(Adapted from Ed Robson, Marsha DeVergilio, and Donna DeButts, *LITSTART: Literacy Strategies for Adult Reading Tutors,* Michigan Literacy, Inc., 1990.)

Activity 51

Understanding Cause and Effect

PURPOSE

To connect reading comprehension and critical thinking skills by identifying causes and effects in text.

METHOD

1. Introduce the concept of cause and effect to the learner by using a practical example. For instance, when Maya decides to go for a walk every day, an effect is that she sleeps better at night.

2. Ask the learner for an example of cause and effect, and help the learner create an example.

3. Select a text that provides a cause-and-effect example.

4. Explain that the learner will be reading about an example of cause and effect.

5. Guide the learner in identifying the cause and the effect in the reading passage.

SUGGESTIONS

- After a learner has read about a relevant topic, spend some time discussing it together. Ask for the learner's opinions on the topic.

- After the learner has practiced identifying cause and effect several times, ask the learner to make a list of causes and effects.

  Example:

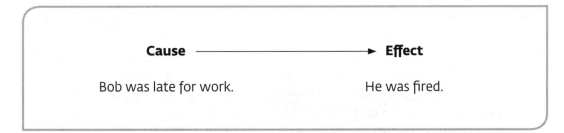

Cause ⎯⎯⎯⎯⎯⟶ **Effect**

Bob was late for work.   He was fired.

- Ask the learner to pick a cause-and-effect example from a list and to write about it in more detail.

Activity 52

Making Inferences and Drawing Conclusions

PURPOSE

To increase reading comprehension by learning to make inferences and draw conclusions from readings.

METHOD

1. Introduce the words *infer* and *inference* to the learner by defining the words and using them in sentences. Explain that to make an inference, a reader needs to look for clues to understand what the author means. The author may not directly say something, but a good reader can draw conclusions and make predictions based on the clues the author provides.

2. Model making an inference about a topic that the learner can relate to. For example, "I read that a tanker just caught on fire on the highway. I can infer that there are going to be traffic delays on that road today. I may draw the conclusion that I won't take that route today."

3. Explain that the learner will be reading a passage and that he or she should make inferences by looking for deeper meaning as he or she reads.

4. Have the learner read several sentences and then stop. Discuss with the learner what he or she has read and inferred.

5. Next, have the learner continue reading several more sentences and discuss the reading and his or her thoughts about it. Continue the process of reading text in small amounts and discussing.

6. After completing the reading, ask the learner what conclusions he or she drew from the text.

SUGGESTIONS

- Learners at any reading level can use their thinking skills to infer and draw conclusions, and there are many ways to practice the skill. You can ask the learner to describe a character or person and then make inferences. For example, "Katy is a high school student. She plays center on the varsity basketball team. What inferences might you make about Katy?" Some inferences might be that she's very tall and practices a lot. The learner may also draw the conclusion that Katy probably practices basketball after school and may not have much free time.

- You can choose an article from *News for You* and ask the learner to make inferences about the person or event described. Ask for a conclusion from the text.

Activity
53 *Using a K-W-L Chart*

PURPOSE

To help the learner to understand and learn from nonfiction readings by setting goals for and keeping track of what he or she already knows, wants to find out, and learns from a reading.

METHOD

Before the reading

1. Prepare a K-W-L chart similar to the sample below.

2. Ask what the learner already knows about the topic of the article. With a beginning reader, jot down ideas in the first column as you and the learner talk.

3. Review the titles, subtitles, photos, and other graphics with the learner.

4. Ask what the learner wants to find out by reading this article. You or the learner then records these questions in the second column.

During the reading

5. Have the learner refer to the K-W-L chart while reading. As questions are answered, you or the learner writes the answers in the third column.

After the reading

6. Have the learner add to the third section whatever information the learner still wants to know about the topic, or you can do that. Discuss where the learner can find that information.

    Example:

Topic/Idea/Title: A Healthy Heart

What I Know	What I Want to Find Out	What I Learned (or Still Want to Learn)
Too much fat is bad for the heart.	How can I cut down on fat in my diet? What foods are bad for the heart?	Red meat and cheese are high in fat. Exercise can help my heart.

(Adapted from D. M. Ogle, "K-W-L: A Teaching Model That Develops Active Reading of Expository Text," *The Reading Teacher*, 39 [1986], 564–570.)

Activity 54

Story Map

PURPOSE

To make a visual outline of a story or article to help the learner understand what he or she has read.

METHOD

Use a graphic organizer to help the learner write about the story and arrange his or her thoughts in a meaningful way.

1. Start by drawing a circle in the middle of the page. Have the learner write the main idea or event in that circle. (Provide assistance if the learner has difficulty writing.)

2. Help the learner map the ideas or events that spring from the center using lines and more circles. Cluster related ideas together.

3. Encourage the learner to look back at the reading selection to see if any important ideas were missed.

Example:

> A learner reads a newspaper article about a proposal submitted by Triangle Construction Company to the city council. The company wants to build a new mall downtown. Bernie Malone, the council president, supported the proposal. Other members expressed concern about the mall's negative impact on the neighborhood, the increased traffic, and the effect on other downtown stores. The company vice president offered to bring a plan for how to handle the traffic to the next council meeting. The council decided to hold a public forum to discuss the mall.

The learner then works with you to create a map similar to the following one.

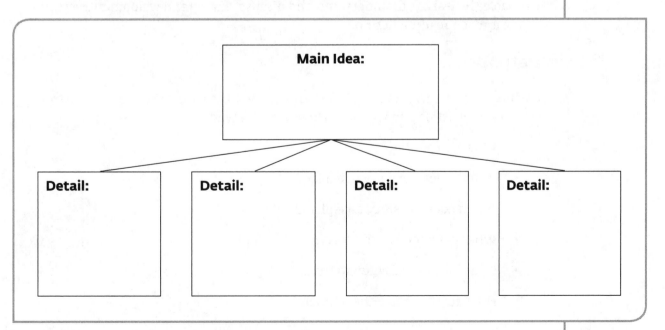

SUGGESTIONS

- When the learner has successfully used a graphic organizer, you can introduce a new graphic organizer for the next reading passage:

Main Idea:

Detail:	Detail:	Detail:	Detail:

- Another graphic organizer that can help learners see what two topics have in common is a Venn diagram. The learner looks for what they have in common and what's unique to each topic. This can also be done comparing characters. See the example below.

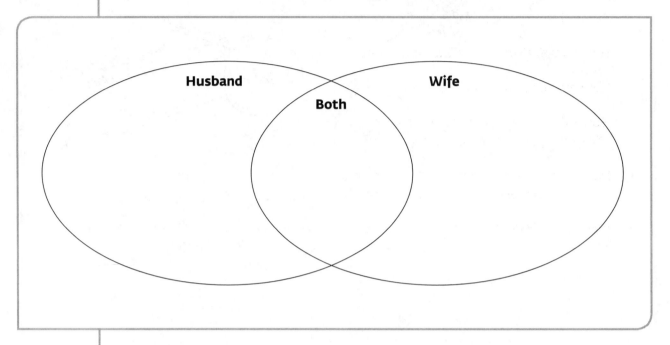

Husband **Both** **Wife**

55 Reading Fiction: *WWWWWH*

PURPOSE

To enable the learner to understand and discuss character development, setting, and plot when reading fiction.

METHOD

1. Introduce the five *W*s and *H*, and explain that the learner should be able to answer questions about each story he or she reads.

    - **W**ho are the characters?

    - **W**here does the story take place?

    - **W**hen does the story take place?

    - **W**hat happened in the story?

    - **W**hy did the character do that?

    - **H**ow did they solve the problem?

2. Use some of the questions or activities below to help the learner to ask and answer *W* and *H* questions.

Who

- What kind of person was _____?

- How do you think the author felt about _____ (a character)?

- How did you feel about _____ (a character)?

- How did _____ (a character) change between the beginning and the end of the story? What caused the change?

- Do you know a person like _____ (a character)? How is he or she like _____ (another character)? Different?

- If you could meet _____ (a character), what do you think you would talk about?

- How are _____ (a character) and _____ (a character) alike in the story? Different?

- Pretend you are _____ (a character). Write (or dictate) a letter to _____ (another character) in the story to say how you feel about him or her.

Where

- Where are the characters when the story begins?

- Close your eyes and picture the setting. Describe what you see.

- Does the story happen in one place or more than one? List all the places.

- Locate the place(s) on a map.

- Have you ever been to a place like _____? What was it like?

When

- When did the story start (year, season, date, time, etc.)? How do you know?

- How much time went by between the beginning of the story and the end?

- Make a timeline for the story. Write the key events on the line in the order in which they happened. Put the earliest event on the left.

- If the story took place at an earlier time in history, what do you think life was like then? What else was happening during that period?

What

- Did you guess how the story would end, or was it a surprise?

- What clues did the author give you that helped you guess how it would end?

- Read cards that describe one key event in the story per card. Put the cards in the order in which the events happened.

- Summarize the story in your own words.

- Pretend you are _____ (a character) in the story. Tell the story as if it happened to you.

- Draw a story map to show what happened in the story (see Activity 54).

Why

- Why did _____ (a character) do that?

- Why did you like or dislike the ending of the story? How would you change it?

- Why did the events in the story happen? List reasons.

- Why did the author choose a word, name, or setting?

How

- How do the characters relate to each other?

- How does one event connect to the next event?

- How does your experience compare with the character's experience?

Activity 56
Signal Words

PURPOSE

To teach learners to recognize signal words so that they can increase their understanding of organization and transitions to improve their comprehension of text.

METHOD

Choose only a few words for each lesson, and include additional practice in following tutoring sessions. Then add more signal words and practice as the learner progresses.

1. Introduce "sequence signals" to the learner. Sequence signals tell the learner that there is an order to the ideas. Some words that denote sequence are *first, second, third, next, before, then, earlier, last, in the first place,* and *after.*

2. Guide the learner to locate signal words in the text.

3. Ask the learner to reread the text to identify the order of events, using the signal words as a guide.

4. Next, introduce the "change-of-direction signals." Change-of-direction signal words or phrases tell the reader that the author is doubling back or jumping forward. Words such as *still, yet, but, while, though, although, however, in contrast, despite, different from, in spite of, conversely, otherwise,* and *on the other hand* are change-of-direction signal words. Guide the learner to locate the words in the reading, and check for understanding.

5. Then introduce the learner to "continuation signals." These words tell the reader that there are more ideas to follow. Words such as *and, also, another, first of all, again, next, too, other, with, furthermore, in addition,* and *similarly* are continuation signals. Guide the learner to locate these words in the reading, and check for understanding.

6. Introduce "conclusion signal words," such as *finally, in summary, from this we see, in conclusion,* and *last of all.* Guide the learner to locate any conclusion signal words in the reading, and check for understanding.

7. Introduce "emphasis signal words," such as *most of all, above all, a major development, the main point, especially important, especially relevant, a central issue,* and *a major event.* Guide the learner to locate these words in the reading, and check for understanding.

SUGGESTIONS

- After the learner is familiar with language experience stories (see Activity 7), ask the learner to retell a story and to add several signal words to denote the order of events.

- Ask the learner to write a three-sentence story using *first, next,* and *then.*

Writing for Meaning

Writing, like speaking, is an opportunity to send a message, to express something to someone else. In order to communicate effectively, writers or speakers have to know who their audience is, what they want to say, and how to say it so that their message is clear to that audience.

Writing is challenging for many people but can be especially intimidating for someone who has never written much more than his or her own name. It can feel risky to begin trying to express yourself in a new way, a way in which you have been silent all your life. Tutors can help by encouraging the learner to first concentrate on meaning: "What would you like to express?" Spelling, punctuation, and grammar will come with practice. Some writing activities, such as cover letters, will require editing, and tutors can assist with that. Spelling, punctuation, and grammar should not be the most important skills for a beginning writer. The learner will be more willing to take chances when you emphasize the strengths instead of the mistakes.

The writing activities (Activities 57–77) provide varying degrees of support for the learner. You can easily adapt any one of these activities to meet the needs of a specific learner. They cover

- letter formation

- copying

- controlled writing

- grammar and structure

- writing instructions and memos

- free writing

Activity 57

Letter Formation: Five Steps to Printing

PURPOSE

To teach printing to learners who have not had much practice using the fine muscles of their hands.

METHOD

1. Select a word that contains the letter the learner wants to work on. Read the word, and review the name and sound of the letter if necessary.

2. First, demonstrate each stroke needed to print the letter. Use your finger to make the strokes in the air or on the desktop. Then ask the learner to do it with you.

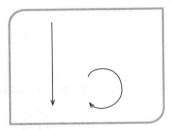

3. Make the strokes on unlined paper. Then ask the learner to copy them.

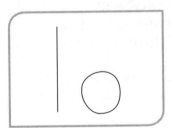

4. Write the whole letter on unlined paper. Describe the letter as you make it. Then ask the learner to print the letter.

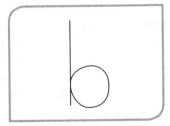

5. Write the letter on lined paper. Use paper with three guidelines. Explain that all letters stand on the bottom guideline. Some letters start from the top guideline

and some from the middle guideline. Some letters descend below the bottom line. Then print the letter on the guidelines, and ask the learner to trace it.

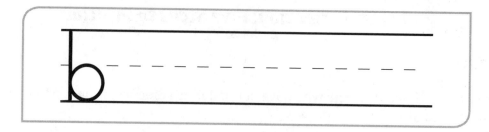

6. Write the letter on lined paper. Ask the learner to use a pencil to practice printing the same letter several times on the guidelines.

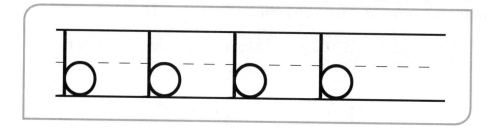

SUGGESTIONS

- Teach only the letters the learner does not know how to write.

- Whenever possible, link the work on writing to the reading that the learning is doing.

- Remember that it isn't necessary to teach the letters in alphabetical order. You might help the learner learn to print the letters in his or her name first, or you can ask if there are letters the learner would like to start with.

- Make sure the learner has plenty of room on the table to write and that the chair and table are at a comfortable height. Be sure there is enough light as well.

- Provide a pencil with an eraser. Many learners do not like to have mistakes or messy papers. The pencil will be easier to use if it has a somewhat dull point, because new writers tend to exert a lot of pressure.

- Limit writing practice for beginners to prevent hand fatigue and cramps. Limit the number of new letters you introduce in each lesson. Review them frequently.

- Keep a sample printing chart (see page 107) on the table for reference until the learner can write all of the letters and numbers independently.

- If he or she is having a lot of difficulty remembering the shape of a letter, ask the learner to describe the shape and relate it to a familiar object as a memory "key."

Examples:

O is round like an orange. J looks like a fishhook.

- If necessary, give extra practice by asking the learner to trace the letters in sand. You can also cut the letters out of sandpaper and ask the learner to trace them with a finger. These techniques are especially helpful for kinesthetic/tactile learners.

- Adapt this process to teach cursive writing after the learner is comfortable and proficient with printing if this is of interest to him or her.

- Explain that letters can look very different depending on the typeface used. To help the learner recognize letters in a different kind of type, select examples of different styles of a letter from magazines or newspapers. Cut them out and paste them on a sheet of paper. Make a separate sheet for each letter. As an alternative, ask the learner to find and cut out these examples.

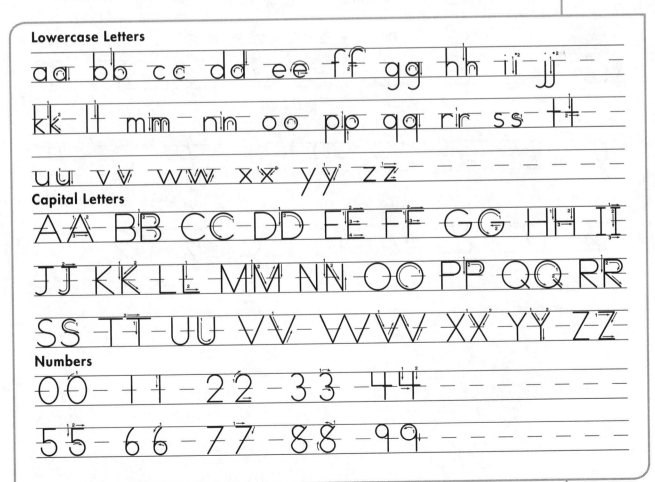

Cursive Letters

Lowercase Letters

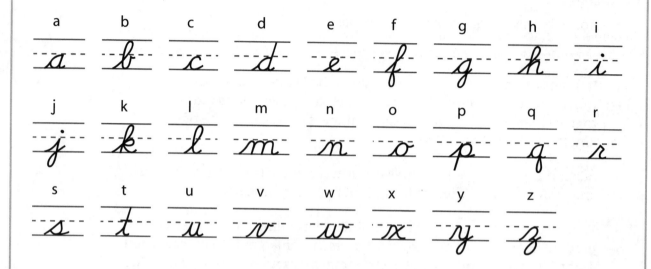

a	b	c	d	e	f	g	h	i
j	k	l	m	n	o	p	q	r
s	t	u	v	w	x	y	z	

Capital Letters

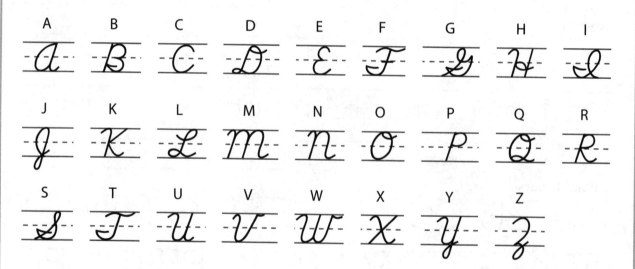

A	B	C	D	E	F	G	H	I
J	K	L	M	N	O	P	Q	R
S	T	U	V	W	X	Y	Z	

Activity 58 — **Copying**

PURPOSE

To help the learner become comfortable with writing words and sentences. (These ideas are nonthreatening and can be done in class or for homework to help the learner develop fine motor skills in a comfortable way.)

SUGGESTIONS

- Ask the learner to read something and circle the words he or she wants to learn to read and write. Ask the learner to copy them onto separate index cards for sight word practice.

- Ask the learner to copy all the traffic signs on his or her street. Then review them together.

- Ask the learner to copy a language experience story that he or she dictated. (See Activity 7.)

- Ask the learner to dictate a note to a friend or relative, copy it, and mail it.

- Help the learner make a vocabulary list related to a text he or she has recently read. Ask the learner to dictate sentences using these words and then to copy the sentences.

- Make a crossword puzzle with words the learner knows. Provide the learner with the list of words, and have him or her write the words where they belong in the puzzle.

- Select activities that reinforce a text that he or she has recently read, or work with topics of interest to the learner.

- Keep copying activities short. Ask the learner to copy only materials that have personal value.

Controlled Writing: Cloze Sentences

PURPOSE

To help a learner who can copy words and sentences begin to use writing to communicate meaning. (Activity 30 shows how to use cloze exercises to develop context skills needed for effective reading.)

SUGGESTIONS

- Ask the learner to complete sentences by selecting missing words from a list of choices.

  Example:

  I asked _____ to get _____ from the store. (bread, Fred)

- Write a list of words and a sample sentence. Ask the learner to write the sentence several times, using a different word in the blank each time.

  Example:

  brother   sister   father   mother   mechanic

  My _____ fixed the brakes on the car.

  My mother fixed the brakes on the car.

- Ask the learner to dictate a description of an experience, a person, or instructions for doing something. For example, ask the learner to give you directions from his or her home to the nearest post office. Then rewrite those directions as a cloze exercise. You may include word choices for each blank.

  Example:

  Turn _____ (right, left) at the light at the corner of Maple and _____ (Grant, Oak). Walk three _____ (blocks, streets). The post office is just past the _____ (laundromat, hardware store).

- Select a paragraph from a passage the learner has read. Rewrite or type it as a cloze exercise. If necessary, provide a list of words from which the learner can choose.

Activity
60

Controlled Writing: Filling Out Forms

PURPOSE

To encourage the learner to use writing to meet practical, everyday needs.

METHOD

1. Collect samples of the types of forms the learner wants to work on (such as employment applications from area businesses or medical forms from a doctor's office). Make copies of the forms you decide to work with so that the learner can practice and won't feel pressure to get everything right on the first try.

2. Work with the learner to fill out one of the forms.

3. Ask the learner to complete another form independently using the information from the one you did together. Provide help as needed.

SUGGESTIONS

- Practice writing checks. Ask a bank for sample checks, or make several copies of a form that looks like a real check. Give the learner a list of bills to be paid. Include the name of the person or company and the amount owed. Ask the learner to write a check for each bill. Provide a reference chart with the number words if needed.

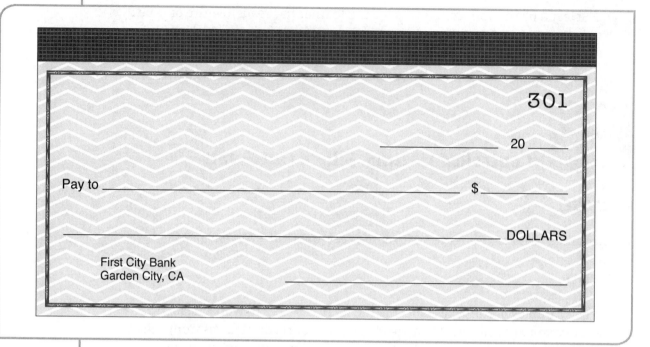

First City Bank
Garden City, CA

- Clip coupons for free samples from newspapers and magazines. Ask the learner to fill them out and mail them in. Then use the product package the company sends as part of a future reading lesson.

- Consider other forms, such as catalog order forms, voter registration forms, library card applications, health history forms, and school permission forms.

- Remember that many forms are now accessible by computer, so the learner may want to complete forms and applications online. The learner will need an email address to fill out most online forms. If he or she doesn't already have one, you can help to set one up. If your program does not have computers or Internet access, talk to your program director or your local librarian to find access to computers and computer instruction, if necessary.

Activity
61

Controlled Writing: Sentence Completion

PURPOSE

To provide structured activities to help the learner begin using writing to communicate ideas.

METHOD

1. Prepare a number of open-ended sentences.

   Examples:

   > When I think of my mother, I feel _____.
   >
   > My favorite color for a car is _____.

2. Ask the learner to copy a sentence beginning and then to complete it with a word or phrase.

3. Ask the learner to read the sentence to you and to explain why he or she selected that word or phrase.

SUGGESTION

Write questions for the learner to answer with complete sentences. To start, select simple literal questions that can be answered with information in the reading selection you are working on. Then move on to more complex or inferential questions that do not necessarily have specific answers. You can also ask the learner questions that require him or her to express an opinion.

Examples:

> When will Soo-Lin arrive home?
> Soo-Lin will arrive at 5:30.
>
> How does Soo-Lin feel about her parents?
> Soo-Lin is angry with her parents.
>
> What is your favorite season?
> My favorite season is summer.

Activity 62

Controlled Writing: Making Lists

PURPOSE

To help the learner write lists both to use as a simple writing activity and to organize ideas or remember important information.

METHOD

1. Ask a question or set a task related to a reading or to the learner's life.

    Examples:

> TO DO
>
> Feed dog
>
> Go to store —
> get milk and eggs
>
> Pick up kids
>
> Make dinner

- List the names of people in your family.
- List the jobs you have held and the dates you worked in them. (*Extension activity:* Organize the list by putting jobs in order of dates.)
- List the names on your holiday gift list and what you will get each person.
- Make a list of chores for family members.
- Make a list of chores to do inside and chores to do outside. (*Extension activity:* Organize the list by using one column or space for inside and one for outside.)
- Make a list of items you need at the grocery store. (*Extension activity:* Organize the list by sorting those items by department: dairy, bakery, produce, etc.)
- Name the tools you need to fix a flat tire.
- Make a list of what you have to do this week. Include the day and time. (*Extension activity:* Organize or sort the list by day or date.)

2. Discuss the list with the learner. Is the list complete? Has anything been left out that should be added? Could the list be reorganized in a way that would make it more useful?

SUGGESTION

Help the learner start keeping a calendar for writing down appointments, meetings, or special events to remember.

Activity 63

Controlled Writing: Basic Organization

PURPOSE

To support learners' abilities to write and organize longer texts.

METHOD

1. Start with a writing topic and organizational structure that are familiar to the learner. An example of a familiar organizational structure is time sequence, what happened first, second, third.

2. If the learner enjoys discussing topics, then talk about the topics together.

3. Ask the learner to complete the structured activity. To begin with, provide sentence starters that use signal words to guide the learner.

4. Ask the learner to read the writing aloud.

5. After practicing writing with this structured frame, give the learner a topic without the sentence starters, and ask him or her to write two or three sentences.

    Example:

Topic: Write about a favorite activity.
Organizational structure: sequential.

In My Free Time

When I have free time, I like to _____. First, I get ready by _____.

Next, I drive to _____. Finally, I enjoy _____

_____.

PURPOSE

To help learners write basic sentences about familiar topics and build their confidence as writers.

METHOD

1. Ask the learner to choose a familiar topic.

2. Ask the learner to write a very short sentence about the topic. Model a short sentence such as "I like coffee."

3. Then ask the learner to write another very short sentence about the topic.

4. Then ask the learner to write several more short sentences about the topic.

5. Finally, suggest that the learner choose one sentence and add to it. For example, "I like coffee with milk."

6. Guide the learner so that the sentence is grammatically correct.

    Example:

TOPIC: FISHING

I like to fish.

I fish in the river.

I fish for bass.

Activity

65

Grammar: Verb Tenses

PURPOSE

To understand and practice using correct verb tenses.

METHOD

Most core reading and writing materials include instruction and practice on grammar.

1. Reusing words that the learner has used in his or her own writing, choose words with regular patterns, and teach simple verb forms first, such as present and simple past tense. Start with regular verbs, such as *work/worked, walk/walked, play/played, start/started, want/wanted/, depart/departed.*

2. Ask the learner to observe the difference between present and past. For example, the *-ed* ending and the different ending sounds.

3. When the learner has become familiar with the ending pattern, begin working on another pattern such as verbs that follow the rule of changing *y* to *i* before adding *-ed*. Use verbs such as *try/tried, study/studied, copy/copied, cry/cried, spy/spied.*

4. Also teach the learner the spelling rule that if there is a vowel before the *y*, it's not usually necessary to change the *y* to *i* before adding *-ed*, such as in *enjoy/enjoyed.*

5. When the learner demonstrates knowledge of regular patterns and reads and writes using the present and simple past, introduce irregular verbs. Start with common verbs, such as *begin/began, build/built, catch/caught, drink/drank, get/got, sell/sold, take/took, make/made.*

6. Follow the same sequence to teach the other tenses. Start with the regular verbs because a large percentage of words follow the pattern, and then teach the irregular verbs.

EXAMPLES OF TENSES

Simple Present: They walk.

Present Perfect: They have walked.

Simple Past: They walked.

Past Perfect: They had walked.

Future: They will walk.

Future Perfect: They will have walked.

Activity 66

Grammar: Parallel Sentence Structure

PURPOSE

To help learners express their ideas in complex sentences with parallel structure and to improve their understanding of text structure when they are reading.

METHOD

1. Model a sentence that includes two verbs that match in form, such as "Tomorrow I want to go *swimming* and *surfing* with my brother."

2. Show the learner the *-ing* endings on both verbs, and explain that this is correct grammar.

3. Ask the learner to make up a similar sentence following the pattern, such as "Tomorrow I want to go _____ and _____ with my brother."

4. When the learner is reading a passage, choose a sentence with correct parallel verbs, and highlight the sentence.

5. Ask the learner to highlight parallel verbs in another sentence.

6. As the learner writes, continue to observe grammatical errors, and plan to include short lessons on grammar rules to help edit his or her writing.

Activity 67

Grammar: Writing Compound Sentences

PURPOSE

To help learners move from writing simple sentences to connecting ideas and writing compound sentences.

METHOD

1. Show the learner two simple sentences that have been combined into one compound sentence. For example: *2 sentences:* She played the guitar. Her friend listened. *1 sentence:* She played the guitar, and her friend listened.

2. Point out the comma and the linking word *and*.

3. Either using the learner's writing from previous lessons or using new sentences, ask the learner to write two sentences and combine them.

4. Ask the learner to read a short passage that has a compound sentence in it, highlighting the sentence and talking about the comma and the linking word.

5. Continue to provide opportunities to practice as needed. Teach the mnemonic FANBOYS to help learners remember linking words: *for, and, nor, but, or, yet, so.*

Activity 68

Building Paragraphs

PURPOSE

To help writers move toward being able to write more extended paragraphs by identifying how a main idea and details build a paragraph.

METHOD

1. Explain to the learner that every reading passage has a main idea and details. (See Activity 54, Story Map.) Each paragraph within a reading passage also has its own main idea and details.

2. In a text the learner has previously read, point out a paragraph, and talk about how the paragraph has a main idea and also details that support the idea.

3. Discuss a topic that the learner wants to write about, and explain that he or she will be writing the main idea of the paragraph and then listing details about the idea.

4. Ask the learner to write a brief description of his or her main idea.

5. Ask the learner to make a list of some details to include in the paragraph.

6. Do this activity several times before the learner writes a paragraph.

7. Have the learner choose one of the main ideas and write a paragraph. Have the learner start by writing a sentence that clearly states the main idea and then follow with a few sentences that mention several of the details he or she listed.

Example:

Main Idea: If I want to save money, I change what I buy.

Details:

- no coffee on the go
- less fast food
- skip going to the movies
- no soda at work
- tell my sons no when they want new toys

Paragraph:

I decided to save money so that I could buy my children new school clothes. I realized it might be hard to save money. I made a plan. I decided to stop buying coffee every day. I skipped going to the movies with my girlfriend. We only go out for dinner once a week now. I'm practicing saying no to new toys for my kids. Though I gave in last week and bought a stuffed dog. In one month I've saved $38.00.

Activity
69 Writing Instructions

PURPOSE

To connect writers' thinking skills and writing skills in a practical activity.

METHOD

1. Show the learner a simple set of instructions, such as the following example. Read the instructions together. Explain that this is an example of written instructions.

Make a peanut butter and jelly sandwich.

1. Get two slices of bread, a jar of peanut butter, a jar of jelly, and a knife.

2. Use the knife to spread peanut butter on one side of one slice of bread.

3. Use the knife to spread jelly on one side of the other slice of bread.

4. Put the bread together with the peanut butter and jelly on the inside.

2. Explain that when writing instructions, it is important not to leave out any steps. It is also important to list the steps in the correct order.

3. Help the learner choose a familiar topic to write about, such as getting his or her children ready for school, preparing to go to a job interview, feeding a pet, or making a pot of coffee. Encourage the learner to choose an activity that he or she does often.

4. Ask the learner to write the first step in the activity and then list the other steps in order.

5. Read the instructions with the learner, and mimic doing each step. Are the instructions correct? Ask the learner if he or she follows the steps whether the activity will be completed correctly.

6. Have the learner add any missing steps or rearrange the order of the steps, if needed.

SUGGESTION

Ask the learner to describe a simple task or activity that he or she performs regularly at work or school. Then have the learner write instructions for a new worker or a new student who needs to complete the same task or activity. Have the learner follow steps 4–6 above, and check the learner's instructions.

Activity

70   *Writing Memos*

PURPOSE

To connect writing to a practical work-related skill.

METHOD

1. Provide the learner with an example of a memo written at a comfortable reading level, or ask the learner to bring in a nonconfidential memo from work.

2. Read the memo together, and point out the headings (*To, From, Date, Subject*) and other features.

3. Create a memo together using a scenario that the learner can relate to.

Sample Scenarios

- The office will be closed for summer break. To prepare for the office to be closed, please clean up your workspace, empty the trash, and make sure your office windows are closed and locked.
- A new receptionist will be starting on January 5th. Please make Rosanna Murray feel welcome by introducing yourself when you see her at the front desk.
- Parents: If you pick up your children after school, please park in the back of the school near the gym doors. Buses will be out front, and parents are no longer allowed to park in front of the school at dismissal time.

---

4. Reread the memo together, and ask the learner to make any changes to clarify the content.

5. When the memo is complete, have the learner sign or initial next to his or her name in the "From" line of the heading.

Example of Memo Components

Headings
To:
From:
Date:
Subject:

Message
Sometimes there is a brief introduction before the body or details of the message.

SUGGESTIONS

- If writing memos is relevant to the learner, add the example of a directive memo during another lesson, and follow the steps in the activity. Here is an example of a directive memo.

Memorandum

To: Project Team 3
From: Paul Gates
Date: August 15, 2013
Subject: Project Schedule

As a result of yesterday's meeting, we will follow the project schedule listed below to prepare for the presentation.

Task	Completion Date
Contact Bureau of Statistics for data	September 9, 2013
Chart the statistics for presentation	September 18, 2013
Prepare presentation slides	September 24, 2013
Practice presentation as a team	September 30, 2013 9AM

- If learner receives memos at work, have him or her bring in a memo to read and discuss.

Activity 71

Free Writing: Journals

PURPOSE

To encourage the new writer to use writing to freely express thoughts and feelings without having to share them with anyone else and without worrying about correct grammar or spelling.

METHOD

1. Have each learner get a separate lined notebook to use for this journal. Some learners may wish to write their journals online. You can find online journal sites by searching for "online journal," or you could help the learner to set up a journal document on his or her own laptop or tablet.

2. Explain that journals or diaries serve as a record of events or as a place to express feelings or ideas. Add that journals are private; the learner shares the journal only if he or she wants to.

3. Provide time in each lesson for the learner to write in the journal. Encourage the learner to make additional entries at home.

4. Tell the learner not to worry about spelling or punctuation. You can answer any questions, or the learner can guess.

5. Explain that an entry can be as short or long as the learner chooses.

6. Suggest topics if necessary.

Examples:

- the weather
- what the learner did during the day
- how the learner feels about the tutoring or what the learner is getting out of it
- something special that happened recently

Journal example:

Jan 4   it is col todda lots of sno.

Jan.7   i got a nu cote it is red

Jan.11   i wen to see the moov Abot 2 pepl livin in the maotins. They mad frends with the wuls.

Jan 14   im doing good I lik reding with Jak. but I don lik writing.

SUGGESTIONS

- Model journaling by writing in a journal while the learner is writing during class.

- Ask the learner to review the journal monthly. Discuss signs of progress. The learner will be able to see how the entries have changed and that writing skills have improved.

Activity 72

Free Writing: Dialogue Journals

PURPOSE

To provide an opportunity for the learner to communicate with another person by means of reading and writing instead of listening and speaking.

METHOD

1. Use a separate lined notebook.

2. Explain to the learner that the dialogue journal is a way to communicate in writing.

3. Begin by writing an entry in the notebook yourself. End it with a question. Ask the learner to answer the question and then write a question for you to answer. Tell the learner not to worry about punctuation, spelling, or grammar.

4. In your response, use correct spelling or punctuation to model something the learner has a problem with. (See the sample on page 126, in which the tutor models the correct spelling of *party* and *years*.) You don't need to call attention to the correction.

5. Regularly look through the dialogue journal with the learner to discuss how his or her writing has improved. You might also mention those improvements in some of your responses in the journal.

SUGGESTIONS

-   Remember that it is important to always respond in some way to the learner's journal comments or questions.

-   Have the learner write in the journal either during the lesson or at home. You can also write in the journal.

-   Share some of yourself in your responses—write about your friends, family, thoughts, and problems.

-   Encourage the learner to discuss favorite books, problems with reading and writing, or things he or she does well.

-   If you are working with a group, ask the learners to work in pairs to create dialogue journals.

Example:

August 10   Bobby is 5 yers ol and wer haveing a parte

My son Mark is 29 years old. Will you get Bobby a present for his party?

A bik with 2 weels

December 13   I'm feeling sad today. My mother is in the hospital. How are you feeling?

I feel god yur mother wat do she hav

December 14   She has cancer and might die. I hope the doctor will have some good news for me today. Do you know anyone with cancer?

December 15   I hope so to cancer is bad. My fend Bill die from cancer He was my fend from wen we wer litle

Activity 73

Free Writing: A Five-Step Process

PURPOSE

To develop a process that allows the learner to communicate clearly and effectively by focusing first on the content and only later on correctness.

METHOD

Rehearse

1. Decide what to write about. Ideas may come from conversation between you and the learner, a practical need (e.g., to write a note to a child's teacher), or thoughts generated from reading. Brainstorming (in Activity 74) and mapping (in Activity 75) are good ways to stimulate or organize ideas. The topic should be something of interest to the learner or should draw on the learner's experience and expertise.

Draft

2. Get it down on paper without worrying about whether it is correct. For the first draft, the learner focuses on the message rather than on punctuation,

grammar, spelling, or handwriting. A learner who has difficulty spelling a word can ask for help or just draw a symbol or picture.

Revise

3. Clarify and expand the content. Help the writer improve the work by discussing it. There are many different approaches you can take:

    • Ask the learner what the piece is about, who the audience is, and what that audience should know, feel, or learn from the writing.

    • Ask the learner to read the piece to you, and then discuss the content. This is especially helpful if the learner is embarrassed about spelling or handwriting. It isn't necessary for anyone else to see the first draft.

      Use the following questions:

      ▷ "Is the topic clear?"

      ▷ "Are there enough supporting details, examples, or reasons?"

      ▷ "Can any details be added, changed, or taken out to make the ideas clearer?"

      ▷ "Are all ideas arranged in a logical order?"

    • Ask the learner to listen critically as you summarize what the learner read or as you read the piece yourself, if the learner wants you to. Then ask, "Did you say what you wanted to say? What do you like best about what you wrote? How can you improve it?"

      Whatever form this feedback session takes, remember to praise. Make suggestions in the form of questions:

      ▷ "What would happen if...?"

      ▷ "How would it sound if...?"

      ▷ "How could you help the reader to better (see, hear, imagine)...?"

      ▷ "How would you summarize in one sentence what you (felt, thought, imagined) when this happened?"

      ▷ "What else did you (notice, feel, say) when this happened?"

      After discussing the draft, the learner may be satisfied with it. If not, the learner can revise the piece as many times as necessary until he or she is satisfied with the content. The learner decides what to change.

Edit

4. Make final improvements or corrections. The learner may revise his or her writing several times. The learner decides when the writing is complete. After the content is satisfactory, the learner can focus on the mechanics—spelling, punctuation, and grammar. The type and amount of editing depend on the purpose of the piece and its audience. A note to a close friend does not need to be edited as strictly as a letter to a possible employer.

   You can help the learner edit the writing by focusing on one thing at a time, perhaps the use of capital letters, periods, or commas. Your task is to help the new writer improve, not to make the writing perfect. Too much editing could undermine a new writer's confidence and feelings of success about writing. Take care not to be overwhelming. (See additional suggestions in Activity 77.)

Publish

5. Share the writing with others. Learners begin to see themselves as writers when they use writing to meet their communication needs and when other people read and react to their ideas and experiences.

   For a new writer, "publishing" a piece means sharing it with another person. It can mean giving a piece to you to read. It can also mean sending a letter or note to someone, posting something on the literacy program's bulletin board, typing and printing out a clean copy, or publishing an item in a newsletter or collection of writings by new writers.

SUGGESTIONS

- This writing process can be used with people who are just learning to write as well as with learners who have more skill. Beginning writers can dictate the first draft as a language experience story. (See Activity 7.)

- A learner who has access to a computer and printer might write, revise, and edit with a simple word processing program.

- This writing process may take several sessions. The writer can also stop the writing process at any time. A learner may no longer be interested in the topic, no longer have a need for the piece of writing, or have a new item to write that is more important. In other words, not every written piece need go through the entire writing process.

- You can keep samples of the learner's writing in a writing folder. Help the learner to see how the writing changes and improves. (See Activity 77.) Remind the learner that writing is a process, not just a product.

Activity 74

Free Writing: Generating Ideas

PURPOSE

To help the learner generate ideas to use in writing. (This activity can be used as part of the rehearsal step in Activity 73.)

METHOD

1. Write a word or topic at the top of a page.

2. Ask the learner to write or dictate as many ideas as possible about this topic.

3. Don't discuss or evaluate any of the ideas. Every idea is valid.

4. When the learner begins to run out of ideas, see if the ideas already listed stimulate other thoughts.

5. When the learner completes the brainstorming, review the list together. Ask the learner to select ideas or topics to use in the writing.

SUGGESTIONS

- If you are working with a group, use brainstorming to generate ideas for writing. Invite people to call out ideas as you write them on the board. Remind them not to comment on any of the ideas until the activity is complete.

- Use a list format or a graphic organizer to organize ideas.

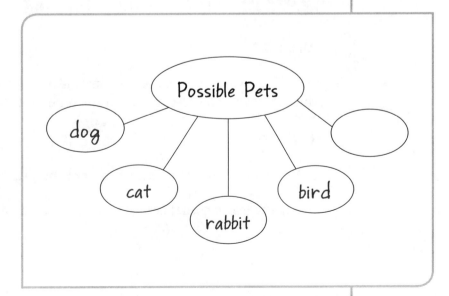

Bad Weather
floods
too cold
too hot
thunderstorms
tornados
hurricanes
fog

- Consider using the simple poem format from *Voyager Book 1, Lesson 2.* This structure guides the writer to find a starting point and add simple personal details. The finished product is a poem.

Instructions: write a poem about yourself

My Poem

Your first name: _____

Four words that tell about you: _____

Son or daughter of: _____

Brother, sister, or friend of: _____

Who feels: _____

Who likes: _____

Who needs: _____

Who lives in: _____

Your last name: _____

Activity 75

Free Writing: Mapping

PURPOSE

To provide a visual image of a person's ideas and how they relate to each other. (This activity can be used as part of the rehearsal step in Activity 73.)

METHOD

1. Write a word or topic in the center of the page, and circle it.

2. Ask the learner what comes to mind when thinking about the topic.

3. Write what the learner says. Group related ideas using circles or lines to show connections.

4. Talk about the finished map, and make additions or revisions.

5. Ask the learner to identify parts of the map to include in the writing.

6. Then have the learner write a short paragraph.

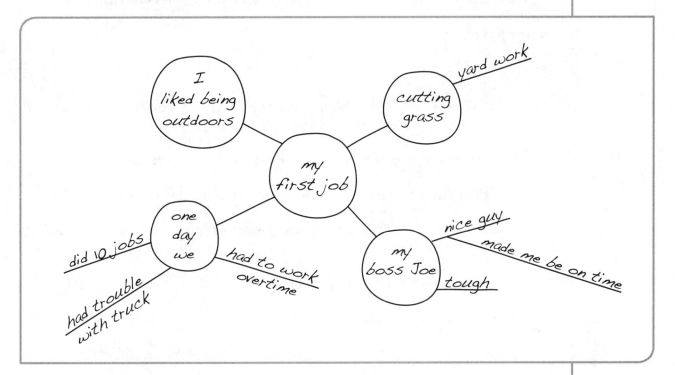

SUGGESTIONS

- For beginning writers, do all the writing, and read the results back to the learner. This frees the learner up to think.

- Try having a more advanced writer do the mapping. You can ask the learner questions to help expand or clarify the map.

- To help the learner get comfortable with maps, work together to make a map of a reading selection you've completed. See Activity 54.

- Ask the learner to brainstorm thoughts about a specific topic and dictate them to you. Go over the list, and ask the learner which ideas belong together. Mark these items or write them in clusters. Then work together to prepare a map. (This procedure gives the learner more control over how the ideas are related.)

Activity 76

Free Writing: Say It a Different Way

PURPOSE

To encourage the learner to explore different forms and styles of writing.

SUGGESTIONS

Have the learner

- take the role of a character in a story he or she just read and write a letter to another character in the story

- select a portion of a fiction story and create a play with dialogue

- write a letter to the editor about an article in the newspaper

- write a news article about a sporting event or something that happened in the community

- write instructions for making something simple

- write a critique of a book or movie

- cut out comic strips from the newspaper, cover the words, and write new ones

- dictate or write a classified ad, a memo, or directions to his or her home

Note: A learner may be uncomfortable with some of these activities. Be sure he or she has enough background or experience before you choose an activity. Does the learner know what a written play looks like? Does the learner know how to read comics? You may want to show some examples of these types of writing and read them together before asking the learner to write in that style.

Activity 77

Keeping a Writing Folder

PURPOSES

- To provide evidence of improvement in a learner's writing.

- To help the learner track improvement in specific skills.

- To help the learner edit future writings independently.

METHOD

1. Choose a folder, three-ring binder, or box for the learner's writings.

2. Make editing notes about the skills you have worked on together. (You can use the inside front cover or separate pages in the folder.) This list should include specific grammar, punctuation, or spelling skills. Add to the list as you identify new things to work on. Choose codes that you and the learner can both use to represent different kinds of errors. (See the example below.)

3. Have the learner review the editing list and use it to correct the next piece of writing.

4. Ask the learner to use the codes to mark other words or places in the writing that might need to be corrected (if the learner isn't sure).

5. Review the learner's work. Mark other uncaught errors that relate to the editing list or to new skills you'd like to focus on. Help the learner make corrections if needed.

6. Work with the learner to decide what to keep in the folder. (See the suggestion below.)

7. Review the folder periodically, and invite the learner to note improvement and what needs more work.

8. Invite the learner to add new pieces or delete old pieces so that the folder reflects progress as he or she sees it. (See "Portfolios" in Chapter 14, "Evaluating Progress," for ideas about using a portfolio to track progress.)

Editing Notes

Spelling
 letter
 understand

Capital letters start a sentence   (T)he keys are in the car.

Punctuation   I am 49.
 sentence ends with a . or ?   How old are you?

SUGGESTION

You might include the following items in the folder. Date each piece so you can see changes or improvements.

- Drafts, revisions, and final copies (stapled together)

- Unfinished pieces (The learner might want to return to these later.)

- Ideas for other writing activities

Improving Spelling

Many learners are intimidated by writing because they don't spell very well. But writing and spelling are two very different tasks. Writing is expressing oneself on paper. Spelling is simply a tool that helps the reader recognize individual words. A good speller is not necessarily a good writer, and some of the best writers are not very good spellers.

Inability to spell should not prevent a learner from beginning to write. Spelling is more important in some situations than in others; it depends on the intended audience. For example, spelling is not too important in a personal journal, but it is very important in a job application.

Follow these general practices in helping learners cope with spelling:

- Set aside some time each week to work on spelling.

- Ask the learner to select words he or she wants or needs to be able to spell. (The words should be from a piece of the learner's writing.) Decide how to teach the words (phonics, word patterns, word parts, etc.). Then create brief exercises that use them. This helps the learner see the relationship between reading and writing.

- Use multisensory teaching techniques. (See pages 26–27.)

- Select words that are already in the learner's listening and speaking vocabularies.

- Select words that were used in a reading selection or the learner's language experience story.

- Select words that the learner uses frequently in writing.

- Encourage the learner to correct his or her own spelling as much as possible, and encourage the learner to recopy the correctly spelled word in its entirety. Rewriting the entire word helps learners remember the correct spelling.

- Look for patterns in the learner's mistakes. Group those words together, and focus on teaching the skill the learner needs. Example: You might help a learner practice writing words that have a silent *w*: *wrinkle, write, wrong, wring.*

    This step is especially important for adults, who will often be judged by their ability to spell words correctly.

For additional work on spelling, see *Focus on Phonics* and *Patterns in Spelling*, published by New Readers Press.

Activity 78
Spelling: Test/Correct/Study/Retest

PURPOSE

To teach the learner a whole-word approach to spelling that encourages self-correcting. (This approach is especially useful for a visual learner.)

METHOD

Test

1. Create a list of five to ten spelling words that the learner wants or needs to know how to spell. The words should be part of the learner's reading, listening, and speaking vocabularies.

2. Say each word, use it in a sentence, and ask the learner to write the word.

Correct

3. Say each word, and spell it out loud so the learner can check the spelling. Have the learner mark any misspelled word.

4. As you spell the word out loud, have the learner write the correct spelling next to the first attempt.

Study

5. Have the learner study only the words that were misspelled. Ask the learner to say the word out loud, spell it out loud, close his or her eyes and visualize the word, look at the word again, cover the word, write it, check it against the correct spelling, and write it again.

Retest

6. Repeat the testing process on the words that were misspelled the first time.

7. Discuss the results with the learner.

Creating a Spelling Dictionary

PURPOSE

To enable a beginning learner who has had trouble using a published dictionary to create a personal dictionary of words he or she needs to write at home or on the job.

METHOD

1. Use a small three-ring notebook (so pages can be added as needed).

2. Write one letter of the alphabet at the top of each page.

3. Encourage the learner to add words that he or she wants to remember how to spell and to consult this dictionary while writing.

4. Ask the learner to write a sample sentence next to the word, if necessary, as a clue to the meaning. This is especially helpful with homonyms.

Examples:

sun	The sun came up.
son	Mike is my son.

SUGGESTION

The spelling dictionary could also have pages for different categories of words (e.g., job application words, family names, words used in school notes, foods, number words, street sign words, or parts list for use in the learner's job).

Activity 80

A Multisensory Approach to Spelling

PURPOSE

To encourage the learner to use as many senses as possible when studying a word to increase the likelihood of remembering how to spell it.

METHOD

Ask the learner to do the following with each word that he or she wants to learn to spell.

kitchen

k	i	t	c	h	e	n

k i t c h e n

1. Look at the word.

2. Say the word.

3. Note the parts that are written the way they sound.

4. Note the parts that are not written the way they sound.

/c/ sound made by *k*
silent *t*
final vowel sound represented by *e*

kitchen

5. Note any special points to remember.

6. Say the word again.

7. Say the letters in sequence—as you look at the word. (If the word has more than one syllable, a beginning student may say the letters for each part of the word as the tutor pronounces that part.)

K-I-T-C-H   E-N

kitchen

8. Look at the word again. Say it.

9. Close your eyes, and see the word in your mind.

K-I-T-C-H-E-N

10. Spell the word aloud as you see it in your mind.

11. Write the word without looking at a model.

12. Check to see if you are right.

SUGGESTION

Neurolinguistic research shows that when people try to picture something in their minds, their eyes tend to move upward. To help a learner improve the ability to visualize and remember how a word looks, write the word on the board for study. You can also write it on a flashcard that you hold above eye level.

13

Pulling It All Together: Lesson Planning

General Principles for Planning Lessons

There are five general principles to keep in mind as you plan your lessons:

1. Lessons should revolve around the learner's goals.

    A learner can travel many different pathways to reach personal goals. Lesson planning involves working with the learner to identify which path works best and what steps need to be taken. A lesson plan is not carved in stone; it is a guide. You need to remain flexible enough to change paths if the learner's needs change or if you find something that works better. Be willing to take some side trips when special needs arise.

2. Lessons should build on each other.

    Build on what the learner already knows when introducing new material. Move from the simple to the more complex.

3. Each lesson should include time for review and reinforcement.

    When you introduce a new concept, plan time in the next lesson to review and reinforce the learning with a variety of activities, such as games, puzzles, flashcards, computer software, and kinesthetic/tactile activities.

4. Each lesson should integrate all four communication tools.

    The learner should use listening, speaking, reading, and writing in every lesson.

5. The learner should learn something new in each lesson.

    Learners need to feel that they are making progress and constantly building on what they know.

The Planning Process

Planning is dynamic. It involves preparing the lesson, doing the lesson with the learner, and evaluating the results. It is not a linear process; rather, it is a series of connected loops, as one lesson leads into another, building on previous material and preparing for lessons to come.

1. Plan the lesson. In preparing each lesson plan, consider these questions:

    • What are the learning objectives? What will the learner accomplish?

    • What materials will you use?

    • What activities and teaching techniques will you use?

    • How can you integrate listening, speaking, reading, and writing in the lesson?

    • How much time will you spend on each activity?

    • How will you and the learner answer the question, "Was it a good lesson?"

2. Preview the lesson for the learner, and do the lesson. Model activities for the learner.

3. Evaluate the lesson. Assess the effectiveness of the lesson by

    • talking with the learner

    • asking the learner to record thoughts in a journal or dialogue journal (See Activities 72 and 73.)

    • making notes in your tutor log (See "Tutor Learning Logs" in Chapter 14, "Evaluating Progress.")

    • writing ideas for the next lesson

Sample Lesson Plans

A learner profile of Robert and two sample lesson plans for him are shown below. The profile includes the last entry in the tutor's log. The two lesson plans are two different ways to design the next lesson. Lesson Plan 1 focuses on the skills taught in the primary instructional series. In Lesson Plan 2, the tutor and learner decide to set the series aside for the moment and focus on the learner's goal of obtaining his commercial driver's license.

LEARNER PROFILE: ROBERT

Personal information
> 23 years old
> Married, expecting first child
> Interests: basketball, playing cards

Previous schooling
> Completed ninth grade

Employment
> Warehouse worker (Heartland Printing)

Long-term goals/needs
> Improve his reading and writing
> Become a delivery truck driver for Heartland

Short-term objectives/needs
> Pass commercial driver's license (CDL) exam
> Find a new apartment for family

Current tutoring information
> Five months in the program
> Meets twice a week for a total of three hours

Primary instructional series
> *Laubach Way to Reading (LWR)*

Last note in tutor's log

9/20/12
Completed Lesson 11 of LWR Book 2. Introduced different spellings for /er/. Worked on basic map-reading skills he will need to make deliveries. Need to review concepts of north, south, east, and west. For homework, he will make a map of his immediate neighborhood.

LESSON PLAN 1

Objectives

- To be able to read the story for *LWR* Book 2, Lesson 12 fluently
- To be able to recognize words with the *-ar* pattern
- To be able to describe the kind of apartment he wants
- To be able to find the newspaper ads for apartments in the neighborhood in which he wants to live
- To be able to recognize 10 commonly used newspaper ad abbreviations (e.g., *bdrm, apt/apts, sec dep, avail immed, incl heat, refrig, full appls, central air, laund rm, off st pkg*)

Plan

Getting settled (5 minutes)

LWR Book 2, Lesson 12 (30 minutes)

- Chart, Story (duet reading), Skills Practice (sections 1, 2)

Check homework (10 minutes)

Break (5 minutes)

Short-term objective: find an apartment (30 minutes)

- List what you want in an apartment: cost, location, etc.
- Use classified ads to locate apartments in preferred location.
- Read sample ads and use flashcards to review abbreviations.

Evaluate lesson: journal entry followed by discussion (5 minutes)

Assign homework (5 minutes)

- Circle apartment ads that meet your requirements.
- Write five questions to ask the landlord.

Review objectives/materials needed for next lesson

LESSON PLAN 2

Objectives

- To review words with different spellings of the /er/ sound pattern
- To understand the content of one section of the CDL manual
- To learn six sight words from that section
- To be able to use mapping to identify what you want to write

Plan

Getting settled (5 minutes)

Check homework (10 minutes)
(or do in class if not completed at home)

Review objectives (2 minutes)

Short-term objective: commercial driver's license manual (50 minutes plus 5-minute break)

- Robert uses table of contents to select section to work on.
- Discuss the topic, and then read it to him.
- LEA: Robert dictates what he wants to remember about this section.
- Identify and practice reading six key sight words from LEA.
- Practice words with /er/ sound.

Writing (10 minutes)

- Map ideas for "Why I want to get my commercial driver's license."

Evaluate lesson by reviewing how well objectives were met (5 minutes)

Assign homework (3 minutes)

- Reread LEA piece.
- Write draft of paragraph using the map about getting CDL.

Review plans for next lesson (5 minutes)

The First Meeting

Tutors and learners are often anxious about the first meeting. With some planning, however, you can help make the learner and yourself more comfortable:

- Make it clear that your purpose is to help the learner learn what he or she wants and needs to know.

- Spend some time getting to know each other. Get to know the learner as an individual. Learn about the learner's life, interests, and goals. Do some initial assessment of strengths and needs. (See "Initial Assessment" in Chapter 4, "Starting Point," for suggestions about how to do an initial assessment.)

- Plan at least one instructional activity. A language experience story can break the ice. You can also supply two or three reading selections at different levels. The learner can choose which to read (or you can read it to the learner).

- Discuss and confirm the time, date, and location of the next lesson.

- Work together to set objectives for the next lesson.

- Discuss the kinds of materials you will be using.

14

Evaluating Progress

The initial assessment (discussed in Chapter 4, "Starting Point") gives you a good starting point for working with a learner. Assessment, however, is an ongoing process that helps measure progress and guides the course of instruction. Three effective tools for evaluating progress are

1.   a portfolio

2.   a tutor learning log

3.   a student learning log

Portfolios

Portfolios have several purposes:

- To document learning and assess progress over time

- To help the learner develop self-evaluation skills by reflecting on the learning

- To demonstrate the variety of reading and writing activities the learner has performed

- To help you and the learner identify needs and plan future lessons

- To show program representatives how the learner is doing (optional)

Guidelines

There is no one right way to compile a portfolio. You can use the following suggestions to help you decide what will work for you:

- Decide what you will keep the portfolio in. This could be a three-ring binder, an accordion file, a file folder, or a box with a lid.

- Collect items to put in the portfolio (e.g., initial assessment information, your observations from the first few weeks of tutoring, or first writing samples) early in the tutoring process so you have baseline information on the learner's starting point.

- Work with the learner to decide what progress you want the portfolio to measure or track.

- Together with the learner, select portfolio items that help you measure progress in selected areas and that represent all the ways the learner uses reading and writing. Make sure all items are dated so you can track change.

- Have the learner periodically add materials so the portfolio reflects continued growth.

- Have the learner write or dictate the reasons for choosing certain items to place in the portfolio and how they reflect his or her literacy development. Include these explanations in the portfolio.

- Every few months, review the contents of the portfolio with the learner to assess progress; identify current needs; and help plan future goals, objectives, and activities. In addition, make notes on how the portfolio shows progress from the baseline or from the last portfolio review.

- Encourage the learner to develop a display portfolio to demonstrate what he or she can do. The learner may choose to share this with anyone: other learners, tutors, program staff, friends, employers, etc. As with an artist's portfolio, the display portfolio consists of samples of the learner's best work.

Evaluating the Portfolio

Consider these questions as you and the learner work together to evaluate a portfolio.

READING PROGRESS

- What has the learner read?

- What can the learner read independently now that the learner could not read independently initially?

- How is the learner using reading to meet personal needs?

- How has the learner's self-image as a reader changed?

- What reading strategies is the learner using?

- What new vocabulary is the learner understanding?

- What level of comprehension is demonstrated?

WRITING PROGRESS

- How many words can the learner write?

- How has the length of the learner's sentences changed?

- How does the learner use punctuation? What punctuation has the learner begun to use correctly?

- How clearly does the learner express ideas? What new vocabulary is the learner using in his or her writing?

- What range of writing tasks has the learner tried?

- How has the learner's self-image as a writer changed?

- How complex is the learner's writing?

- How legible is the learner's printing or handwriting?

Materials to Include in a Portfolio

Learners and tutors must work together to decide what to include in the portfolio to reflect the learner's progress. The following are some examples of what you might include:

- Writing samples

- Lists of books read (with brief descriptions or evaluations)

- Lists of new ways learner uses reading and writing

- Learner log (see "Student Learning Logs" in this chapter)

- Learner's reflections on the portfolio pieces

- Photocopies of selected journal or dialogue journal pages (see Activities 59 and 60)

- Printing and cursive writing samples

- Language experience stories

- Audio recordings of learner reading aloud

- Checkups or periodic tests that are part of a published instructional series

- Descriptions of reading strategies learner is using

- Published writings

- Samples of real-life materials learner has read or written (e.g., recipes, application forms, letters)

- Works in progress

- Lists of specialized sight word vocabulary learner has mastered

- Items that show development in writing style, organization, clarity, or word choice

- Samples of first and final drafts that show idea development and self-editing

- Goal statements

Tutor Learning Logs

A tutor or teacher log (see example on page 150) is an ongoing record of the tutoring process. After each lesson, you make notes about

- things that the learner worked on

- areas that were discussed during the lesson evaluation

- things that you observed as the learner did the planned activities or used the materials

- the learner's strengths and needs

- ideas for future instruction

- stories or experiences the learner described that illustrate how the learner's skills are improving or the impact tutoring is having on the learner

- your thoughts about the tutoring process—how you are growing and changing

You then review these notes periodically to determine

- how the learner has improved

- what the learner needs to work on

- what types of materials or activities seemed to work best

Tutors can choose to share some of the notes with the learner as appropriate.

Example of Tutor Log

6/6

Finishing up with Challenger 2. Began work on the final review chapter today. I was really thrilled to see how easily she read the vocab. words she had learned and how she could tell me basic info. about the story the words were taken from. Really impressed she retained so much of what she'd read weeks ago.

Seems to have excellent comprehension when reading, but has difficulty interpreting instructions for exercises. We usually review instructions together and if it seems she does not get the homework instructions, we go over them and do sample exercises. Seems that if she doesn't follow through with homework soon after our lesson, she gets confused about exercises and doesn't finish them. I would like to boost her confidence. Maybe I'll prepare a special sheet of instructions with a few exercises to work on together in class.

6/10

Liz's concentration was low tonight—repeatedly misread words she should not have difficulty with. Had trouble seeing the difference between r and n. When she had difficulty pronouncing a word, I asked her to sound out letters and to see if the letter was r or n. I didn't know what to do. It really seems like she can't see the difference between the two letters. Will talk to program director or another tutor to see if they have any suggestions.

6/13

Another tutor suggested creating paragraphs using short words with r and n and having Liz circle words containing one letter and underlining ones that have the other. I'm going to try to see if she will confuse the two if her task is to concentrate on seeing r or n.

Liz and Fred are planning to drive to California for vacation. I worry because they are both literacy students and there are a lot of things that can happen on a road trip to California! Not to mention the undependability of their car. Still, they're excited and enthusiastic, so Liz and I did some work and made some plans related to her trip. She wants to

- review a U.S. map and GPS information
- plot out a route they might take
- set up a trip journal to keep her working on her writing skills
- select a fiction book to read on the trip

TEACHING ADULTS: A LITERACY RESOURCE BOOK

Student Learning Logs

When the learner is ready, you can encourage the learner to keep a log or journal to track learning progress. The learner can write about what he or she is learning and his or her feelings about it. The learner can also write about things learned outside of tutoring. Tutors should periodically allow time in the lesson for the learner to reflect on learning and make an entry in the log. You can suggest topics, such as

- what I worked on during the lesson

- what I have learned in the past two weeks

- what I think about the lesson

- what I need to work on

- ideas for future lesson activities

Sample Learner Goals

The checklist on pages 153–155 includes some of the goals of new readers in adult literacy programs. Tutors and learners can use the checklist to help them establish their own goals. There are 10 general categories:

1. General skills

2. Transportation

3. Money

4. Jobs

5. Government/law

6. Health

7. Food

8. Children

9. Recreation

10. Religion

A good place to begin is by asking learners which categories they would like to review. Tutors can assist learners in reading these sections if necessary and then ask the learners to indicate how each column should be checked. Tutors should encourage learners to add other goals that are important to the learners.

If the learner identifies a specific goal, take some time to find out more about the learner's interest or needs. For example, if the learner wants to read a newspaper, what parts are of greatest interest? If the learner wants to be able to write letters, what is the purpose, and who is the audience?

	I do it well enough	I want to work on it	I don't need to work on this now
General Skills			
Write my name, address, and telephone number			
Write other people's names, addresses, and telephone numbers			
Tell time			
Read a calendar			
Write down appointments			
Use a telephone book			
Read street signs			
Read store names and signs			
Read or write a letter or note			
Read a newspaper			
Read a magazine			
Read a book			
Use a dictionary			
Other:			
Transportation			
Read bus or train schedules			
Read traffic signs			
Read a driver's manual			
Read maps			
Read a car maintenance/repair manual			
Other:			
Money			
Read pricing labels in stores			
Write checks or money orders			
Read a bank statement			
Read and pay bills			
Fill out an application for a credit card			
Fill out public assistance forms			

	I do it well enough	I want to work on it	I don't need to work on this now
Fill out unemployment forms			
Fill out tax forms			
Other:			
Jobs			
Read job ads			
Fill out a job application			
Read job-related manuals/forms			
Write a résumé			
Read information on paychecks			
Read charts, graphs, or diagrams			
Read contracts			
Fill out order forms			
Make lists			
Write reports			
Other:			
Government/Law			
Read an election ballot			
Read leases			
Read legal documents/forms			
Read about government or history			
Other:			
Health			
Read a thermometer			
Read labels/directions on medicine bottles			
Read warning/poison labels			
Read about what to do for injuries or sicknesses			
Fill out medical or dental insurance forms			
Read about staying healthy			
Read about pregnancy and childbirth			
Read about AIDS or other diseases/health problems			
Other:			

	I do it well enough	I want to work on it	I don't need to work on this now
Food			
Write a shopping list			
Read grocery ads			
Read coupons			
Read food labels			
Read recipes			
Read menus			
Other:			
Children			
Read books to children			
Read school notices and reports			
Fill out school forms			
Write notes to the school			
Write a medical history/record of shots			
Read about child care			
Other:			
Recreation			
Read a TV or radio program schedule			
Read a movie schedule/movie reviews			
Read words to songs			
Read notices or newsletters about community activities			
Read directions or rules for playing games			
Fill out an application for a library card			
Other:			
Religion			
Read church bulletins			
Read the Bible or other religious materials			
Read aloud during religious services			
Other			

B Sample Criteria for Evaluating Materials

People use many different criteria when choosing instructional materials for beginning readers. The list below includes some of the criteria you might consider as you try to select appropriate materials for a specific learner. Which criteria you decide to use will also depend on the type of materials and their purpose (to build or reinforce skills, to present information, or to entertain).

As you work together, encourage the learner to evaluate the materials or suggest others. Remember that the real test of the effectiveness of material is not whether it meets the criteria presented here but whether it meets the needs of the learner.

Print Materials for the Learner

Content (Text and Illustrations)

- Is relevant to the learner's

  - ▷ goals
  - ▷ needs
  - ▷ interests
  - ▷ experiences
  - ▷ values
  - ▷ culture

- Is adult-oriented, or addresses adult goals (e.g., children's books that the learner wants to be able to read to children or grandchildren)

- Helps build positive self-image in the learner

- Doesn't assume previous knowledge or experience that the learner doesn't have

- Doesn't promote stereotypes

- Is free from bias (cultural, religious, ethnic, racial, class, sexual, etc.)

- Contains accurate, up-to-date information

- Presents information in a logical sequence, building from the known to the unknown

- Is written at an appropriate reading level if the learner will use it independently

- Contains enjoyable reading selections that motivate the learner to read more

- Uses a writing style appropriate for the learner

- Contains graphics (photos, illustrations, charts) that enhance the text and do not confuse or distract the learner

Additional Content Criteria for Published Instructional Materials

- Contains clear explanations of any new skills or concepts

- Provides adequate opportunity for practicing and reinforcing skills

- Provides feedback to the learner on how he or she is doing

- Encourages the learner to apply the skills and information in real-life contexts

- When appropriate, contains clear directions and adequate support for the tutor or teacher

Format

- Is adult in appearance

- Has appropriate typeface and type size

- Has appropriate line length (not too short or too long) for the type size

- Has adequate spacing between the lines of type

- Uses color to enhance readability (In general, type should be black on white paper for greatest contrast and ease of reading.)

- Appears inviting and easy to read:

    ▷ graphics or subheads to break up solid text

    ▷ adequate use of white space

- Has clear graphics (pictures, charts, illustrations) that are near the relevant text

- Has cover, photos, and illustrations that are appropriate for the learner

Computer Software for the Learner

Many of the above criteria can also be used to evaluate instructional software. Some other characteristics to look for in software include the following:

- Is easy to learn (user-friendly) for a person unfamiliar with computers or keyboarding skills

- Has clear learning objectives

- Has on-screen directions that are clear and can be read by the learner

- If appropriate, has an authoring system that allows the tutor to tailor instruction to individual needs

- Has text, graphics, and music (if any) that are adult-oriented

- Requires active learner participation and interaction

- Includes sufficient practice of any new concept being taught

- Has a way to record where the learner leaves off and an easy way for the learner to get back to that place

- Provides feedback to the learner and the tutor on how well the learner is doing and what areas need more work

- Allows the learner to control the rate and sequence of the program

- Has audio that sounds natural and is easy to understand

- If desired, has a learner-management or record-keeping system to track learner progress

Teacher's Guides

Many of the same criteria used for evaluating learner materials also apply to teacher's guides. In addition, you should consider the following:

- Contains clear directions

- Is designed so that the tutor or teacher can find information quickly and easily

- Contains directions for how to place a learner in the materials

- Describes how to adapt the materials to meet individual needs

- Includes a way to check the learner's progress and needs

300 Most Frequently Used Words

The following 300 words make up 65 percent of all written material.
The words are listed in their order of frequency.

1. the	26. or	51. will	76. number	101. over
2. of	27. one	52. up	77. no	102. new
3. and	28. had	53. other	78. way	103. sound
4. a	29. by	54. about	79. could	104. take
5. to	30. word	55. out	80. people	105. only
6. in	31. but	56. many	81. my	106. little
7. is	32. not	57. then	82. than	107. work
8. you	33. what	58. them	83. first	108. know
9. that	34. all	59. these	84. water	109. place
10. it	35. were	60. so	85. been	110. year
11. he	36. we	61. some	86. call	111. live
12. was	37. when	62. her	87. who	112. me
13. for	38. your	63. would	88. oil	113. back
14. on	39. can	64. make	89. its	114. give
15. are	40. said	65. like	90. now	115. most
16. as	41. there	66. him	91. find	116. very
17. with	42. use	67. into	92. long	117. after
18. his	43. an	68. time	93. down	118. thing
19. they	44. each	69. has	94. day	119. our
20. I	45. which	70. look	95. did	120. just
21. at	46. she	71. two	96. get	121. name
22. be	47. do	72. more	97. come	122. good
23. this	48. how	73. write	98. made	123. sentence
24. have	49. their	74. go	99. may	124. man
25. from	50. if	75. see	100. part	125. think

126.	say	161.	such	196.	still	231.	along	266.	four
127.	great	162.	because	197.	learn	232.	might	267.	carry
128.	where	163.	turn	198.	should	233.	close	268.	state
129.	help	164.	here	199.	America	234.	something	269.	once
130.	through	165.	why	200.	world	235.	seem	270.	book
131.	much	166.	ask	201.	high	236.	next	271.	hear
132.	before	167.	went	202.	every	237.	hard	272.	stop
133.	line	168.	men	203.	near	238.	open	273.	without
134.	right	169.	read	204.	add	239.	example	274.	second
135.	too	170.	need	205.	food	240.	begin	275.	later
136.	mean	171.	land	206.	between	241.	life	276.	miss
137.	old	172.	different	207.	own	242.	always	277.	idea
138.	any	173.	home	208.	below	243.	those	278.	enough
139.	same	174.	us	209.	country	244.	both	279.	eat
140.	tell	175.	move	210.	plant	245.	paper	280.	face
141.	boy	176.	try	211.	last	246.	together	281.	watch
142.	follow	177.	kind	212.	school	247.	got	282.	far
143.	came	178.	hand	213.	father	248.	group	283.	Indian
144.	want	179.	picture	214.	keep	249.	often	284.	really
145.	show	180.	again	215.	tree	250.	run	285.	almost
146.	also	181.	change	216.	never	251.	important	286.	let
147.	around	182.	off	217.	start	252.	until	287.	above
148.	form	183.	play	218.	city	253.	children	288.	girl
149.	three	184.	spell	219.	earth	254.	side	289.	sometimes
150.	small	185.	air	220.	eye	255.	feet	290.	mountain
151.	set	186.	away	221.	light	256.	car	291.	cut
152.	put	187.	animal	222.	thought	257.	mile	292.	young
153.	end	188.	house	223.	head	258.	night	293.	talk
154.	does	189.	point	224.	under	259.	walk	294.	soon
155.	another	190.	page	225.	story	260.	white	295.	list
156.	well	191.	letter	226.	saw	261.	sea	296.	song
157.	large	192.	mother	227.	left	262.	began	297.	being
158.	must	193.	answer	228.	don't	263.	grow	298.	leave
159.	big	194.	found	229.	few	264.	took	299.	family
160.	even	195.	study	230.	while	265.	river	300.	it's

(From Elizabeth Sakiey and Edward Fry, *3000 Instant Words*, Jamestown Publishers, Highland Park, NJ, rev. ed., 1984.)

160

TEACHING ADULTS: A LITERACY RESOURCE BOOK

Social Sight Words

A
Adults Only
Ask Attendant for Key
B
Beware
Beware of the Dog
Bus Stop
C
Caution
Closed
Condemned
D
Danger
Dentist
Doctor (Dr.)
Do Not Cross
Do Not Enter
Do Not Refreeze
Don't Walk
Down
E
Elevator
Emergency Exit
Employees Only
Entrance
Exit
Exit Only
F
Fire Escape
Fire Extinguisher
First Aid
Fragile
G
Gentlemen
H
Handle with Care
Hands Off
Help
High Voltage
I
In
Inflammable
Information
Instructions
K
Keep Away
Keep Closed at All Times
Keep Off (the Grass)
Keep Out
L
Ladies
Last Chance for Gas
Listen
Live Wires
Look
M
Men
Men Working
N
Next Window
No Admittance
No Checks Cashed
No Credit
No Credit Cards Accepted
No Dogs Allowed
No Dumping
No Fires
No Fishing
No Hunting
No Loitering
No Minors
No Smoking
No Smoking Area
No Spitting
No Swimming
No Trespassing
Nurse
O
Office
Open
Out
Out of Order
P
Pedestrians Prohibited
Police Station
Post No Bills
Post Office
Private
Private Property
Pull
Push
R
Rest Rooms
S
Smoking Prohibited
Step Down
Stop
T
This End Up
This Side Up
U
Use Before [Date]
Use Other Door
V
Violators Will Be Prosecuted
W
Walk
Wanted
Warning
Watch Your Step
Wet Paint
Women

How to Make Speech Sounds

Adult learners need to be able to use the sounds of letters as one tool to help them recognize printed words. Being able to identify the sounds in a word they hear will also help learners spell the word.

Tutors and teachers can use the chart on pages 163–167 for several purposes:

- To check which sounds the learner already knows and which ones to work on, you can do one of the following:

  ▷ Cover everything on the page except the first column, and ask the learner to make the sound for each letter or letter combination as you point to it.

  ▷ Point to the word in the second column. Ask the learner to read it (or read it yourself), and then ask the learner to make the sound for the letter(s) in bold type. This will not tell you if the learner knows the sound in isolation, but it will tell you if he or she has the concept of sounds. Note that you can also substitute words of your own choosing for those in column 2.

- To help describe how a sound is made (if the learner is having difficulty producing it)

- As a reference to the variety of ways that a sound can be spelled

There are four stages in the production of any speech sound:

1. Put lips in position.

2. Produce the sound.

3. Stop the sound.

4. Relax position.

The following codes are used to describe the sounds in the chart.

Vocalization (Voc.) codes (used in column 4):

    v = voiced (vocal cords vibrate)

    un = unvoiced (vocal cords do not vibrate)

    c = continuant (sound can be continued as long as the speaker has breath)

    s = stop (sound can't be continued)

    n = nasal (sound comes through the nose)

Frequency codes (used in column 1):

    [1] = primary or most common sound for a spelling

    [2] = secondary sound for spelling

Primary Spelling	Secondary Spellings	As In	Voc. Code	Articulatory Position
b	-	bird	v s	Stop air with lips together; open with small puff of breath. Voiced equivalent of /p/.
c	 k ck ch	cup kitchen kick Chris	un s	Tongue tip down, back of tongue touching lower teeth. Stop air with hump or arch of tongue, and emit breath from back of throat. Unvoiced equivalent of /g/.
d	-	dish	v s	Lips and teeth slightly parted. Stop air with tongue tip touching roof of mouth just behind upper teeth. Tongue is dropped as breath is expelled. Voiced equivalent of /t/.
f	 ph gh	fish phone tough	un c	Lower lip touching upper teeth lightly. Unvoiced equivalent of /v/.
g	-	girl	v s	Tongue tip down, touching back of lower teeth. Stop air with hump or arch of tongue, and emit breath from back of throat. Voiced equivalent of /k/ or /c/ above.
h	-	hand	un c	Has no position of its own. Position tongue for vowel following it, and give breath sound.

Primary Spelling	Secondary Spellings	As In	Voc. Code	Articulatory Position
j		jumping	v	It is combination of /d/ and /zh/. Lips forward. Start with tongue tip up. Lower as breath is expelled. Voiced equivalent of /ch/.
	g(e)	gentle		
	g(i)	ginger		
	g(y)	gym		
k		kitchen	un	Same as /c/ above.
	c	cup	s	
	ck	kick		
	ch	Chris		
l	-	leg	v	Tongue tip touches just behind upper teeth. Air comes out along side(s) of tongue.
			c	
m	-	man	v	Lips together. It is made with same lip position as /b/ and /p/, but /b/ and /p/ are stops.
			n	
			c	
n		neck	v	Lips and teeth slightly parted. Tongue tip touching roof of mouth just behind upper teeth. Lower surface of tongue shows. It touches gum ridge with tongue position like /t/ and /d/, but /t/ and /d/ are stops.
	kn	knock	n	
	gn	gnaw	c	
p	-	pan	un	Stop air with lips together; open with big puff of breath. Unvoiced equivalent of /b/.
			s	
r		river	v	Tongue tip up. Lips forward and almost squared. Round lips before voicing.
	wr	wrap	c	
s		snake	un	Teeth close but not touching. Tongue tip down. Unvoiced equivalent of /z/.
	c(e)	cent	c	
	c(i)	city		
	c(y)	bicycle		
t	-	tent	un	Lips and teeth slightly parted. Stop air with tongue tip up touching roof of mouth just behind upper teeth. Lower surface of tongue shows. Tongue is dropped as breath is expelled. Unvoiced equivalent of /d/.
			s	
v	-	valley	v	Lower lip touching upper teeth lightly. Voiced equivalent of /f/.
			c	
w	-	woman	v	Lips forward and rounded, with one-finger-wide opening, as with *oo* in *room*.
			c	

Primary Spelling	Secondary Spellings	As In	Voc. Code	Articulatory Position
y	-	yells	v c	Lips drawn back, teeth close together, as with /ee/.
z	 s	zipper his	v c	Teeth close but not touching. Tongue tip down. Voiced equivalent of /s/.
a	-	apple	v c	Wide jaw opening. Tongue down.
e	 ea	egg/Ed head	v c	Lips and teeth slightly closer together than for /a/.
i	 y	in city	v c	Lips and teeth slightly closer together than for /e/.
o	-	olive	v c	Wide jaw opening. Prolong sound.
u	-	up	v c	Medium jaw opening. Relaxed lips. Prolong slightly.
x	-	box	un	Teach as /ks/.
qu	-	quarter	un	Teach as /kw/. Lips rounded like *oo* as in *room*.
th[2]	-	thanks	un c	Tongue touches both upper and lower teeth. Unvoiced equivalent of /th[1]/ below. Consonant digraph.
sh	 ch	shop Chicago	un c	Lips forward and squared. Teeth close but not touching. Tongue down. Tongue has wider groove than in /s/ sound. Unvoiced equivalent of /zh/ as in *measure*. Consonant digraph.
ch	- tch	children kitchen	un c	A combination of /t/ and /sh/. Lips forward. Start with tongue tip up; lower as breath is expelled. Unvoiced equivalent of /j/. Consonant digraph.
wh	-	whistle	un c	Teach as /hw/ or /w/. Consonant digraph.
th[1]	-	mother the	v c	Voiced equivalent of /th[2]/ above. Consonant digraph.
ar	-	arms	v c	Teach according to person's local pronunciation.

Primary Spelling	Secondary Spellings	As In	Voc. Code	Articulatory Position
ur		burn	v	Tongue tip down. Lips forward, almost squared, more relaxed than for /r/.
	er	her	c	
	ir	girl		
ng	-	ring	v	Tongue tip down behind lower teeth. Hump or arch tongue. Nasal equivalent of /k/ or /g/. Consonant digraph.
			n	
			c	
a-e		cake	v	Teeth about half inch apart. Hold twice as long as /ē/. Tongue down.
	ai	paint	c	
	ay	day		
	a	paper		
i-e		five	v	Jaw wide at start, then move to narrower opening.
	igh	night	c	
	y	spy		
	ie	tie		
	i	I		
ee		three	v	Lips drawn back, teeth close together. Hold twice as long as /ĭ/.
	ea	eat	c	
	e	we		
	ey	key		
	e-e	Pete		
o-e		nose	v	Lips forward and rounded, with two-finger-wide opening.
	oa	boat	c	
	ow	snow		
	o	go		
or	-	York	v	Lips forward with three-finger-wide opening.
			c	
oo		book	v	Lips forward, almost squared.
	ou(ld)	would	c	
oo		food	v	Lips forward and rounded, with one-finger-wide opening. Prolong sound.
	u-e	June	c	
	ue	blue		
	ew	chew		

TEACHING ADULTS: A LITERACY RESOURCE BOOK

Primary Spelling	Secondary Spellings	As In	Voc. Code	Articulatory Position
aw		lawn	v	Lips forward, with three-finger-wide opening.
	au	Paul	c	
	a(ll)	ball		
	augh(t)	caught		
	ough(t)	bought		
u-e		huge	v	Teach as /ee/ plus *oo* as in *room*.
	u	pupil	c	
	ew	few		
	ue	argue		
ou		mountain	v	Combination of /o/ plus *oo* as in *room*. Start with wide jaw opening, move lips forward with small opening.
	ow	town	c	
oi		oil	v	Combination of /aw/ and /i/. Start with lips forward for /aw/, then draw back for /i/.
	oy	boy	c	
su		measure	v	/zh/. Voiced equivalent of /sh/.
	si	television	c	

Common Phonics Elements and Principles in English

Consonants

Consonant Letters That Represent One Sound

b	bed	k	kite	p	pen	v	vase
d	dime	l	lake	qu	queen	w	woman
f	feet	m	man	r	rope	y	you
h	hat	n	name	t	ten	z	zoo
j	job						

Consonant Letters with More Than One Sound

s	sun, rose	Note:	*s* can sound like /s/ or /z/
x	six, example, xylophone		*x* can sound like /ks/, /gz/, or /z/
c	can, cop, cup cent, city, icy	Rule:	*c* followed by *a, o,* or *u* sounds like /k/ *c* followed by *e, i,* or *y* sounds like /s/
g	gas, got, gum ginger, germ, gym get, give, fogy	Rule:	*g* followed by *a, o,* or *u* sounds like /g/ *g* followed by *e, i,* or *y* can sound like /j/ *g* followed by *e, i,* or *y* can also sound like /g/
gu	guard, guess, guilt, guy	Rule:	*gu* followed by a vowel sounds like /g/ *u* is usually silent

Consonant Blends

Consonant blends are two or three consonants (or a consonant and digraph) that commonly occur together. Each sound can be heard.

	Initial Blends				Final Blends			
bl	blue	shr	shrunk	ct	act	rb	curb
br	bride	sk	skate	ft	left	rce	force
chr	Christmas	sl	sleep	ld	gold	rd	card
cl	clock	sm	smart	lf	self	rf	scarf
cr	cry	sn	snow	lk	milk	rk	bark
dr	drop	sp	spoon	lm	film	rl	girl
fl	flame	spl	split	lp	help	rm	farm
fr	friend	spr	spring	lt	melt	rn	corn
gl	glass	squ	square	mp	lamp	rp	burp
gr	groom	st	step	nce	chance	rse	course
pl	plate	str	street	nch	lunch	rt	smart
pr	price	sw	swim	nd	hand	sk	ask
sc	scar	thr	throw	nge	range	sp	clasp
sch	school	tr	track	nse	sense	st	last
scr	scream	tw	twin	nt	front	xt	next
				pt	kept		

Consonant Digraphs

Consonant digraphs are two consonants that represent one sound.

ch	chair, machine, Christmas	sh	she
ng	ring	th	thing, the
nk	bank	wh	whale, who
ph	phone		

Silent Consonant Combinations

These are common consonant combinations that contain one or more silent letters. Hyphens indicate initial or final combinations.

-ck	clock		-mb	climb
gh	high, rough, ghost		-mn	autumn
-ght	sight, thought		rh-	rhyme
gn	sign, gnat		sc-	scent
kn-	know		-tch	catch
-lk	talk		wr-	wrong
-lm	calm			

Vowels

Vowel Letters and the Sounds They Represent

Each vowel letter represents several vowel sounds. The most common sounds are represented in the words listed below. All vowels can represent the schwa sound in unstressed syllables. The schwa is represented in many dictionaries by the symbol /ə/.

	Short Sound	Long Sound	Other Sounds	Schwa Sound
a	man	name	all, father, water	**a**bout
e	bed	me	cafe	op**e**n
i	six	time	ski	Apr**i**l
o	job	go	son, do, dog	sec**o**nd
u	but	rule, fuse	put	aw**fu**l
y	gym	fly	any	

Vowel Combinations and the Sounds They Represent

Listed below are common vowel digraphs or vowel-consonant combinations. Many of these combinations produce long vowel sounds. If a combination represents more than one sound, a key word is given for each common sound.

Long Vowel Sounds

ai	rain		ie	field, pie
ay	day		igh	high
ea	meat, great		ind	find
ee	feet		oa	soap
ei	either, vein		oe	toe
eigh	eight		oo	food
eu	feud		ue	due
ew	blew, few		ui	fruit
ey	key, they			

Other Vowel Sounds

ai	against		oo	book, blood
au	auto		ou	you, country, out, soul, could
aw	saw		ough	though, thought, through, enough, bough, cough
augh	taught, laugh		ow	own, town
ea	head		ui	build
oi	boil			
oy	boy			

r-Controlled and *l*-Controlled Vowels

When vowels are followed by *r* or *l*, the pronunciation of the vowel is usually affected.

air	fair	err	berry	ur	fur, fury
ar	car, dollar, warm	ir	girl	urr	purr
arr	carry	irr	mirror	al	pal, bald
are	care	oar	roar	all	ball
ear	ear, earth, bear	oor	door	ild	mild
eer	deer	or	horse, word, color	ol	old, roll, solve, doll
er	very, her	our	hour, four, journal	ull	full, dull
ere	here, were, there				

Other Vowel-Consonant Combinations and the Sounds They Represent

-dge	badge	-ci-	magician, social
-ed	hated, rubbed, fixed	-si-	session, television, Asian
-gue	league	-ti-	caution, question, initial
-que	antique	su	sugar, measure
-stle	whistle	-tu-	picture

Common Syllable Patterns in English

Some patterns of letters in syllables signal short vowel sounds. Others usually produce long vowel sounds. Recognizing the common short- and long-vowel syllable patterns can aid in decoding and spelling unknown words. It is usually the letter or letters that follow a vowel that determine pronunciation.

Key: V = any vowel
      C = any consonant
      (C) = may or may not be a consonant

Syllables That Usually Produce Short Vowel Sounds

Closed syllables (syllables that end with one or more consonants)

VC: at, Ed, is, on, up

CVC (also called 1-1-1 syllables): had, let, did, lot, but

CVCC: hand, less, with, lock, bump

Exceptions: find, child, high, sign, old, poll, bolt, most

Syllables That Usually Produce Long Vowel Sounds

VCe (silent *e* syllables): name, eve, time, hope, rule

VV(C) (double vowel syllables): paid, need, meat, die, boat, due, food

(C)V (open syllables): ta/ble, fe/male, bi/cycle, go, o/pen

Exceptions (many unaccented open syllables): a/muse, to/day

A Syllable That Usually Produces the Schwa

Cle (consonant followed by *le*): table /tā/bəl/, gentle /gĕn/təl/

Rules for Adding Endings

The Doubling Rules

1. If a word has one syllable, one vowel, and one final consonant, double the final consonant before adding an ending that starts with a vowel. Do not double a final *w* or *x*. (This is also called the 1-1-1 Rule.)

Examples:

> hop + ed = hopped
> run + ing = running
>
> *but*
>
> fix + ed = fixed
> row + ing = rowing

2. If a word has more than one syllable, double the final consonant if the last syllable has one vowel, has one final consonant, and is accented and the ending starts with a vowel.

Examples:

> forgót + en = forgotten
> begín + ing = beginning
>
> *but*
>
> offer + ing = offering

The Silent e Rule

If a word ends in silent *e*, drop the final *e* before adding an ending that starts with a vowel.

Examples:

> joke + ing = joking
>
> secure + ity = security

The y to i Conversion

If a word ends in a consonant plus *y* (Cy), change the *y* to *i* before adding an ending, unless the ending starts with *i*. Note that this rule does not apply when a vowel precedes the *y*.

Examples:

lucky + er = luckier
happy + ness = happiness

but

cry + ing = crying

Rules for Pronouncing the Endings

Endings -ed *and* -d

1. Pronounce as /d/ if preceded by a vowel sound or the voiced consonant sounds /b/, /g/, /j/, /l/, /m/, /n/, /ng/, /th/, /v/, /z/, /zh/, or /r/.

    Examples:

tried	mailed	bathed
robbed	tamed	moved
tagged	rained	razed
raged	hanged	starred

    But some words that end in the sounds /l/, /m/, and /n/ can add either *-ed* or *-t*. Note that adding *-t* might change the sound of the root word.

    Examples:

spelled/spelt	dreamed/dreamt	burned/burnt

2. Pronounce as /ed/ if preceded by the sound /d/ or /t/.

    Examples:

kidded	posted

3. Pronounce as /t/ if preceded by the unvoiced consonant sounds /ch/, /f/, /k/, /p/, /s/, /sh/, or /th/.

Examples:

reached	tapped
stuffed	kissed
coughed	cashed
picked	toothed

Ending -s

1. Pronounce as /z/ if preceded by a vowel sound or a voiced consonant sound.

Examples:

fleas   cans   ribs   saves

2. Pronounce as /s/ if preceded by an unvoiced consonant sound.

Examples:

packs   laughs   eats

Ending -es

1. Pronounce as /z/ if preceded by a vowel sound or a voiced consonant sound.

Examples:

cries   calves

2. Pronounce as /iz/ if preceded by an unvoiced consonant sound.

Examples:

benches   kisses   fishes   fixes

Sample Word Patterns

For suggestions about how to teach word patterns as a word recognition strategy, see Activity 27. The list below is a sampling of some of the word patterns in English with examples of one-syllable words that contain those patterns. When teaching patterns, be careful not to mix words that have similar spellings but different sounds (*brown, blown*).

| a | pack | rag | sail | shake | ram |
| | track | tag | trail | take | swam |

ab	**ad**	**age**	**ain**	**ale**	**ame**
cab	bad	cage	gain	male	blame
gab	glad	page	pain	pale	came
grab	had	rage	rain	sale	flame
stab	lad	stage	stain	scale	name
tab	mad	wage	train	tale	same

ace	**ade**	**aid**	**air**	**all**	**an**
face	grade	braid	chair	ball	bran
grace	made	laid	fair	call	can
lace	shade	maid	hair	fall	Dan
place	trade	paid	pair	small	man
trace	wade	raid	stair	tall	pan

ack	**ag**	**ail**	**ake**	**am**	**and**
back	bag	fail	bake	ham	band
black	drag	mail	brake	jam	hand
crack	flag	pail	cake	Pam	land

sand
stand

ane
cane
Jane
lane
plane
sane

ank
bank
clank
crank
sank
tank

ap
clap
lap
map
nap
snap

ape
cape
drape
grape
scrape
shape

are
care
fare
flare
rare
share

ash
bash
cash
dash
flash
mash

ass
bass
brass
class
glass
grass

ast
blast
cast
fast
last
past

at
bat
cat
chat
hat
that

atch
hatch
latch
match
patch
scratch

ate
fate
gate
late

plate
state

ave
brave
cave
gave
grave
save

ay
day
pay
play
say
stay

aze
blaze
daze
gaze
haze
maze

e

each
bleach
peach
preach
reach
teach

eak
creak
leak
sneak
speak

weak

eal
deal
heal
meal
real
steal

eam
beam
cream
dream
scream
team

ean
bean
clean
Jean
lean
mean

ear
clear
fear
hear
near
year

eat
beat
cheat
heat
meat
wheat

eck
check

deck
neck
peck
speck

ed
bed
Fred
red
shed
wed

eed
bleed
feed
greed
need
weed

eek
cheek
creek
Greek
peek
week

eel
feel
heel
kneel
steel
wheel

een
green
queen
screen
seen
teen

eep
creep
deep
jeep
keep
sleep

eet
beet
feet
greet
meet
sweet

ell
bell
fell
sell
spell
tell

en
den
hen
men
pen
ten

end
bend
mend
send
tend
trend

ent
bent
cent
rent

sent
went

ess
dress
guess
less
mess
press

est
best
nest
pest
test
west

et
bet
get
met
pet
set

i

ice
mice
nice
price
rice
twice

ick
chick
pick
sick
thick

tick

id
bid
did
hid
kid
skid

ide
bride
hide
pride
ride
slide

ift
drift
gift
lift
shift
sift

ig
big
dig
pig
rig
wig

ike
bike
hike
like
Mike
strike

ile
file
mile

pile
smile
while

ill
bill
fill
hill
spill
still

im
brim
dim
him
Jim
rim

ime
crime
dime
grime
slime
time

in
chin
fin
pin
sin
tin

ind
bind
blind
find
kind
mind

ine
fine
line
mine
shine
spine

ing
bring
king
ring
sing
sting

ink
blink
drink
pink
sink
wink

ip
chip
dip
hip
lip
trip

ipe
gripe
ripe
stripe
swipe
wipe

ire
fire
hire
sire
tire

wire

iss
bliss
hiss
kiss
miss
Swiss

it
bit
fit
grit
hit
sit

itch
ditch
glitch
pitch
stitch
witch

ite
bite
kite
quite
white
write

o

oat
boat
coat
float
gloat
throat

ob
Bob
cob
job
mob
rob

ock
block
clock
lock
rock
sock

od
God
nod
pod
rod
sod

og
bog
fog
hog
log
smog

oke
broke
joke
poke
smoke
spoke

old
cold
gold
hold
scold

sold

ole
hole
mole
role
stole
whole

one
bone
lone
phone
stone
zone

ool
cool
fool
school
spool
tool

oom
bloom
boom
doom
gloom
room

oon
croon
loon
moon
noon
soon

oop
coop

droop
hoop
scoop
stoop

oot
boot
hoot
loot
root
shoot

op
chop
cop
hop
mop
stop

ope
cope
hope
rope
scope
slope

ore
chore
core
more
shore
store

ose
chose
close
hose
nose
those

oss
boss
cross
loss
moss
toss

ot
got
hot
knot
lot
spot

ought
bought
brought
fought
sought
thought

ound
found
mound
pound
round
sound

owl
fowl
growl
howl
prowl
scowl

own
blown
flown
grown

shown
thrown

own
brown
clown
crown
down
frown

u

ub
cub
hub
rub
stub
tub

uck
buck
duck
luck
struck
truck

ud
bud
cud
dud
mud
stud

uff
bluff
cuff
huff
puff

stuff

ug
bug
drug
dug
jug
snug

ull
dull
gull
lull
mull
skull

um
bum
chum
gum
hum
sum

ump
bump
clump
dump
jump
lump

un
bun
fun
gun
run
sun

unch
bunch

crunch
lunch
munch
punch

ung
hung
lung
rung
stung
sung

unk
chunk
drunk
dunk
junk
sunk

unt
bunt
hunt
punt
runt
stunt

ush
blush
gush
hush
mush
rush

ut
but
cut
hut
nut
shut

(Adapted from Tim Brown and Deborah F. Knight, *Patterns in Spelling*, New Readers Press, 1990.)

TEACHING ADULTS: A LITERACY RESOURCE BOOK

Compound Words

afternoon	broadcast	downstairs	grasshopper
airline	bulldog	downtown	haircut
airmail	buttercup	dragonfly	handcuff
airport	buttermilk	drawbridge	handlebar
anchorman	campfire	drive-in	hangup
anchorwoman	carpool	driveway	hardware
another	cattail	dropout	haystack
applesauce	classmate	drugstore	headache
ashtray	clipboard	earring	headlight
backyard	clothesline	earthquake	headquarters
bareback	clothespin	eyeball	highway
barefoot	copout	ferryboat	holdup
baseball	copperhead	filmstrip	homemade
basketball	copyright	fireplace	jellyfish
bathroom	cowboy	flashback	landlady
bedspread	crosswalk	flashcube	landlord
billfold	cupboard	flashlight	leftover
birthday	cupcake	folklore	lifeboat
blackbird	cutout	football	lifeguard
blackboard	daydream	frogman	lipstick
blackout	daytime	frostbite	lookout
bloodhound	dishpan	fruitcake	loudspeaker
blueprint	doorknob	gentleman	midnight
bookkeeper	doorway	goldenrod	moonship
breakfast	downpour	goldfish	moonwalk

motorcycle
newsboy
newscast
newspaper
newsprint
nightgown
notebook
nutcracker
oatmeal
offbeat
outboard
outcome
outfield
outfit
outlaws
outstanding
overalls
overcoat
overlook
overpass
pancake
paperback
payoff
peanut
peppermint
pigtail
pinball
pinpoint
playmate

playpen
ponytail
popcorn
postcard
postman
pushover
quicksand
railroad
railway
rainbow
rattlesnake
rawhide
redwood
ripoff
rowboat
runway
sailboat
sandpaper
scarecrow
screwball
screwdriver
shipwreck
shoelace
shortstop
sidewalk
silverware
skateboard
skyscraper
slipcover

snowdrift
snowfall
softball
splashdown
spotlight
starfish
streetcar
suitcase
sunbeam
sunflower
sunrise
sunset
sunshine
sweatshirt
sweetheart
teacup
textbook
Thanksgiving
thumbtack
thunderstorm
timetable
tiptoe
toenail
toothbrush
toothpick
touchdown
tugboat
turntable
turtleneck

undercover
underground
understand
undertake
uproot
uptown
vineyard
volleyball
washcloth
wastebasket
watchman
watercolor
waterfall
waterfront
watermelon
weatherman
weekend
whirlpool
wholesale
wildcat
windmill
windpipe
windshield
wiretapping
woodland
woodpecker
wristwatch

(From Edward Bernard Fry, Jacqueline E Kress, and Dona Lee Fountoukidis, *The Reading Teacher's Book of Lists*, Prentice Hall, Paramus, NJ, 1993.)

TEACHING ADULTS: A LITERACY RESOURCE BOOK

Prefixes and Suffixes

Prefixes

a-
without; on, in; in a state of

ad-, ac-, af-, al-, ap-, as-, at-
toward, to, near, in

anti-
against, opposing

auto-, aut-
self

bi-
two

con-, col-, com-, cor-
with, together

contra-
against

de-
reverse, remove, reduce

di-
separation, twoness

dis-, dif-
absence; opposite; reverse, remove

ex-, ef-, e-
out of, from

in-, im-
in

in-, im-, il-, ir-
not

inter-
between, among

intra-
inside, within

intro-
in, inward

mis-
wrongly, badly

mono-, mon-
one, alone

multi-
much, many

ob-, oc-, of-, op-
toward, against

per-
through, thoroughly

poly-
much, many

post-
after, later; behind

pre-
before

pro-
forth, forward

re-
back, again, anew

sub-, sup-, suc-, suf-
under; lesser

super-, sur-
superior, above; additional

trans-
across

tri-
three

un-
not, opposite of; reverse an action

uni-
one

Suffixes

-able
able to, capable of, liable to

-age
action or result of an action; collection; state

-al
relating to, characterized by

-ance, -ancy
state or quality of; action

-ant
inclined to; being in a state of; someone who

-ate
cause, make; state, condition; someone who

-en
made of; cause to be or have; become

-ence, -ency
state or quality of; action

-ent
inclined to; being in a state of; someone who

-er
more

-er, -or
someone who; something that

-ery, -ary, -ory, -ry
place where; collection, condition, or practice of

-est
most

-ful
full of

-hood
state, quality, or condition of

-ial
relating to, characterized by

-ian
person who; of, relating to, belonging to

-ible
able to, capable of, liable of

-ic
relating to, characterized by

-ice
state or quality of

-ine
of, pertaining to; chemical substance

-ion
act, result, state of

-ious
full of, characterized by

-ism
act, condition, doctrine, or practice of

-ist
someone who

-ite
quality of; follower or resident of; mineral product

-ive
performing or tending toward an action

-ize
cause to be or become

-less
without, lacking

-ly
in the manner of

-ment
state, act, or process of

-ness
state, quality, or condition of

-ous
full of, characterized by

-ship
state, quality, or condition of; skill

-ty, -ity
state or quality of

-ure
act, process; function or body performing a function

-ward
direction

-y
characterized by

(From Tim Brown and Deborah F. Knight, *Structures in Spelling*, New Readers Press, 1990.)

Academic Vocabulary

Kindergarten	1st Grade	2nd Grade
Alphabet	Blend	Adjective
Author	Capitalization	Adverb
Illustrator	Character	Pronoun
Beginning	Setting	Dictionary
Ending	Consonant	Encyclopedia
Consonant	Vowel sound	Fiction
Vowel	Fantasy	Nonfiction
Drawing	Illustrate	Folktale
Fairy tale	Sequence	Fable
Letter	Predict	Discussion
Letter-sound relationship	Punctuation (e.g., comma, quotation mark)	Main idea
Picture book	Question	Message
Poem	Statement	Predicting
Story	Reality	Prewrite
Song	Syllable	Draft
Print	Vocabulary	Edit
Retell	Media (e.g., book, video, film, illustration)	Publish
Rhyme	Summarize	Author's purpose
Sentence	Information	Table of contents
Speech	Noun	Glossary
Title	Verb	Singular
Uppercase (capital)	Compound word	Plural
Lowercase		Plot
Word		Punctuation (e.g., comma, semicolon)
Period		Base (root) word
Question mark		Prefix
Exclamation mark		Suffix
Read		

(From *A Guide for Tennessee Educators*, Tennessee Department of Education, July 2006, revised July 2009.)

Banking- and Work-Related Vocabulary

Internet searches by occupation will also provide tutors with lists of words specific to occupations. Additionally, learners who are preparing for job interviews benefit from learning and practicing job interview–related vocabulary, planning for the experience, and role-playing their answers to interview questions.

Words for Banking

account

bank statement

bankrupt

borrow

budget

cash

cashier

check

credit (card)

currency

debt

deposit

exchange rate

interest (rate)

invest

investment

lend

loan

mortgage

owe

pay

save

savings

share

withdraw

General Work Words

application (form)

commuter

computer

employee

employee handbook

employee orientation

employer

entry-level position

job

job interview

job training

occupation

organize

perform

produce

profession

salary

skilled worker

test

training

training course

update

vacancy

wage

Health-Related Vocabulary

Adults have a need to read and understand health vocabulary so that they can communicate and make effective decisions regarding health care for themselves and their families. Although there are thousands of health-related words, here is a sampling of words that may be important for learners. Learners can add their own health words to their personal dictionaries.

ache	clean	experience
active	collapse	family
alcohol	coordination	flexible
anemia	cure	fracture
appetite	dehydration	gain
bacteria	depression	gland
behavior	diagnostic	growth
blood	diet	harmful
blood pressure	disorder	headache
body	doctor	health
bone	drinking	healthy
breath	drug	heart
breathe	eat	high blood pressure
calcium	eating	hormone
calorie	emotion	hygiene
cardiac	emotional	immunity
change	energy	immunization
circulation	exercise	improve

individual

infection

ingredient

injury

insurance

involuntary

iron

jog

joint

jump

lifestyle

lumbar

medical

medicine

nurse

panic

participation

perspiration

pharmacy

physiotherapy

play

portion

positive

practice

pregnancy

prenatal

pressure

prevention

protect

puncture

radiation

recovery

relationship

relaxation

respiration

safety

skin

sleep

strength

stress

support

therapy

ultrasound

vaccination

vitamin

walk

walking

weight

x-ray

yoga

zinc